Loving NIGERIA

kepressng

NIGERIA | UK

First Published in 2024

The moral rights of the authors has been asserted.
Individual contributions ©2024

This book is sold subject to the condition that it shall not, by way of trade or otherwise, be lent, re-sold, hired out, or otherwise circulated without the publisher's prior written consent in any form of binding or cover other than that it is published and without a similar condition including this condition being imposed on the subsequent purchaser.

Kemka Ezinwo Press Ltd (KEP) has no control over or responsibility for any author, third-party websites, or articles that may be referred to in or on this book.

A CIP catalogue record for this book is available from the Nigerian National Library & the British Library.

ISBN: 978-978-76996-1-4 (Paperback)
ISBN: 978-978-76996-2-1 (E-Book)

This novel is entirely a work of fiction. The names, characters, and incidents portrayed in it are the work of the author's imagination. Any resemblance to actual persons, living or dead, events or localities is entirely coincidental.

Typeset by Kepressng Ltd
Cover illustrated by Louisa Vision Arts & designed by Agnes Kay-E

Dedications

To those rooted like the iroko tree,
In the belief of Nigeria's new dawn,
Whose spirits carry the flame,
Of unity beyond their dreams
May your faith be our guiding star.

To hearts that pulse with loyalty and pride,
That the independence once earned,
Was not just in name.
Our skin, Mother Earth's unshorn mystery,
Will soon receive her reward.

To patriots who strike their chest in determination,
May the tripod rivers of Niger and Benue;
Rooted in cursive veins of the mangrove
Remain fierce and free.
And your silver horses neigh strong on the green.

Like the eagle,
The constancy of Mother Earth,
Nigeria will rise and soar!

- *Agnes Kay-E*

Some stories in this collection have been previously published in various anthologies and literary journals. Their original appearances are as follows:

"The List" in *The Condom & Other Stories* by Peter Chika
"Black & Blue" in *Rebirth*.by Kepressng
"Ogu" in *Ogu & Other Stories* by Kepressng
"Mother'd My Girls" in *Notes on Love & Other Stories* by Kepressng
"The S. O. S." in *Notes on Love & Other Stories* by Kepressng
"Children of Chukwu" in *Notes on Love & Other Stories* by Kepressng
"Austin Tries to Do Better" on *The Medium*.
"Tito" in *Oops!* by Kepressng
"The Unforgettable Christmas" in *Ogu & Other Stories* by Kepressng

I am grateful for the opportunity to share these stories with a new audience in this collection.

Table of Contents

Author's Note	vi
The List	1
Black and Blue	20
Heartbeats & Blueprints	42
Ogu	78
Marriage on the Brink	90
Mother'd My Girls	112
The Bus Trip	125
The S. O. S.	133
Wildfire	154
Flappy Wings of Freedom	175
Children of Chukwu	198
Austin Tries to Do Better	209
Tito	229
The Unforgettable Christmas	244
The Missing Part	252
Contacts	279
About Us	281
Other KEP Titles	282
2026 COMPETITION!	283

Author's Note

The past couple of years have presented exceptional challenges for Nigerians, casting a shadow over our pride and sense of identity. At times, it might seem as though we have lost touch with our renowned ability to shape real and imagined worlds. However, even in the face of adversity, our spirit and creativity shine brightly.

On August 18, 2024, driven by an impulse, I invited short stories from Nigerian authors, setting a tight two-week deadline to release the collection on Independence Day, October 1. I wasn't certain it would yield. The outcome amazed me. I received an extraordinary array of multi-genre stories—each one a hard-hitting, thought-provoking, and explorative narrative that is worthy of celebration.

I am immensely proud of these authors and the remarkable body of work they have contributed. What started as a spur-of-the-moment idea has blossomed into a collection. These stories celebrate our Nigerian*ness* and evoke emotional depth without resorting to palliative literature—a testament to our resilience and our unyielding capacity to thrive, regardless of what is thrown at us.

This collection is a powerful reminder of our enduring strength in storytelling.

Also, to anyone who feels overlooked or underestimated, remember: you are a star in your own right. It is simply a matter of recognising and embracing your inherent brilliance.

- *Agnes Kay-E*

The List

Peter Chika

Osita watched his opponent snore. It was now well past 2:00 a.m., and Uche Emengo, the Great Iroko, was stretched out on the sofa, his expansive stomach spilling over the edge. The snoring began as a rattle somewhere in the recesses of that belly and reached a high-pitched crescendo before petering out in a low rumble. At times, it seemed from the sound that the snorer was suffocating. Osita ruminated on how that might solve the problem, if the Great Iroko expired then and there from natural causes. The decision would be wrested from the men of "timber and calibre" currently huddled in the anteroom. Osita Anumba, PhD, former university lecturer, would be the sole candidate for chairman of the Adimora local government council.

Osita would be the first to admit that it was hardship that had driven him into seeking electoral office. One did not need uncommon vision to know that the pay for lecturers was awful. For how long could he continue to eke out a living by selling lecture notes to supplement his meagre income? He was tormented by the endless sniggering and smirking of his students, particularly the girls who all had sugar daddies, many of whom were politicians and elected officials. A stint in government was the surest route to fabulous wealth in these parts—only a fool could argue with that. Osita had finally accepted that he'd been rather foolish, having railed in vain against VIPs—vagabonds in power—for years.

And so, quelling the last of his petulant demons, he'd decided to try his hand at the grassroots. He was overqualified to be a councillor, but the council chairmanship would do nicely. The way it worked, chairmen had complete control of local government funds, which meant that they could divert most of the money to their personal accounts. None of them passed up the chance. The little left—and it was very little indeed—they shared among their councillors and patrons.

The current chairman, the expansive Right Honourable Sam Okanku, Knight of Saint John, MPA (honoris causa), had campaigned for election with the slogan, "Operation Cleanup," promising to introduce accountability and good governance. He would make a show during campaign rallies of sweeping the stage with a broom as a picturesque metaphor for his mantra. Now, a few months before the expiration of his term in office, he was simply called "Cleanout" for the treatment he had meted out to the local government's coffers.

The council did nothing more than run after petty traders and subsistence farmers for taxes while waiting for windfalls from the central government. Still, the people did not revolt. Instead, like feudal serfs, they scrambled for handouts from the very people who kept them in penury. Despite the irreverent nickname that he had attracted, Cleanout was a loveable rogue rather than a loathed villain. Small crowds gathered outside his house every day for the cash gifts he doled out. He was easily one of the most popular men in the local government area. It was strange, but Osita had also given up on wondering about it.

The last straw for Osita had come when he'd taken up the matter, on the sidelines of an academic conference, with a well-known professor of politics. Osita had expected a lively conversation, peppered with the ideas of philosophers like Gramsci and Mazrui. To his dismay, the other man had refused to engage. "He for whom the pear has ripened, let him eat," said the political scientist. "One day, it might be your turn or my turn to eat."

Osita had been surprised at how receptive the political parties were. He'd first approached the Labor Party, which was regarded as the party of intellectuals, but quickly realised that they had no real presence in the local government area. He'd then talked with the Amalgamated Peoples' Congress, the main national opposition party. Their pitch was appealing, but he was gruffly advised by his father that a party formed by people from across the Niger could never win an election in these parts. "If you want to tie those people like a wrapper around you," said the old man, "you might as well consider yourself naked."

He had learnt the hard way to listen to his father, who always wanted him to study medicine. He'd opted for microbiology in a moment of adolescent rebellion and watched with regret as less stellar classmates went on to become affluent medical doctors.

Osita had settled on the ruling party, the Progressives Democratic Party. A combination of circumstances worked in his favour. The PDP rotated electoral offices between the six villages—or "autonomous communities" as they liked to call themselves—that made up the Adimora local government. It was the turn of his village to produce the next candidate for chairman.

The first problem was that he was not a registered member of the party. The PDP's constitution said a person had to have been a member for at least a year to be qualified for nomination. It was a despondent Osita that went to register, thinking that he had to postpone his ambitions until he was qualified.

Registration was the province of the party secretary in each electoral ward. It turned out that Osita's ward secretary was a former student of his. Patrick Kaneme had heard of Osita's political intentions and was effusive about helping. He issued Osita a backdated registration card.

"B-b-but," stuttered Osita, "won't they check?"

Patrick laughed. "Check what, sir? It is what I give them that they will take. Welcome to politics, sir!"

Osita suppressed his guilt. At least he had not bribed to get the backdated card.

He was now a bona fide member and eligible for the party's primaries. The next problem was money. Osita had none. It was Patrick to the rescue again.

Patrick took him to Chief Onwuka, the richest man and ultimate power broker in the local government area. Onwuka was barely literate but had proved an astute businessman. He had worked his way up from bus conductor to owner of the biggest transport company east of the River Niger. Everybody seeking elections from the six villages—nay, autonomous communities—approached him for money, and he gave according to how serious he judged the candidacy.

In times past, you paid your respects to a potential patron with kola nuts and palm wine. Nowadays, you went with the most expensive cognac. At Patrick's urging, a nervous Osita cleared most of his savings to buy the case of XO that they now presented to Chief Onwuka, both supplicants bowing extremely low.

"So *dokinta*, you are wanting to do election; you are wanting to be our chairman, *ndeh*," said Onwuka. "You must to not go there and thief, are you hearing me?"

Osita was relieved. There were rumours that local government chairmen delivered ten percent of the council's monthly revenues to Chief Onwuka to retain his support. Onwuka's admonition against stealing flew in the face of such stories. Osita immediately warmed to this rotund millionaire.

Chief Onwuka said he liked the idea of a doctor - *dokinta* - aspiring to be the local government chairman. He lamented, without a hint of irony, that uneducated people—"those who are not go school"—had dominated Adimora council elections in the past. He gave Osita five million naira in cash, for starters, to fund the campaign. Osita had never seen such money in one place before. The amount meant that Chief Onwuka thought him to be a potential election winner. Things were falling into place faster and better than he had imagined.

Patrick became his campaign manager and organised his first rally. Osita researched the local government's statistics vigorously, drawing on his university connections. He prepared the kind of socialist manifesto he'd always yearned to hear, but never did, from election candidates in the country. He was going to introduce the villagers to the sort of rousing campaign speeches that CNN and BBC showed to be the norm in Western countries.

To Osita's consternation, he was interrupted with howls of derision early into his delivery and then pelted with water sachets. Patrick, who'd stood bemused throughout, called him aside after.

"My chairman, sir, you are not in the university anymore. Our people, the ones who will actually vote, are simple people and most of them did not finish school. I have to show you something, my chairman."

As was conventional, Patrick and Osita's growing band of acolytes had taken to addressing him by the title of the position he was contesting for. To do any different would mean that you did not believe Osita was going to win the elections, and that would immediately rank you, in Chief Onwuka's diction, a "betraitor."

Patrick dragged Osita off to watch, from a safe distance, a rally by his opponent for the PDP nomination. Uche Emengo, the Great Iroko, was a former thug. He had been a local government councillor several times already. His belly expanded a few more inches during each term he served. He now decided that he was going for the jugular. "Oche Iroko" was his campaign slogan which yielded the double entendre "strong chair" and "Iroko's chairmanship."

Unlike Osita, who had spoken English, the Great Iroko addressed his rally in Igbo. He delved straight into promises of free everything—free primary and secondary education, free water boreholes in every compound, free health centres in every village. Every month, his administration would give a bag of rice and a tin of palm oil to every widow in the area. The local government would employ all unemployed youths. No explanation was proffered on how the council's limited finances would cope with even a fraction of these, but the gathering lapped it up.

The Great Iroko spiced his disjointed speech with traditional proverbs, some of them barbs directed at Osita. Midway into the rambling, Iroko's retinue lifted him onto their shoulders and carried him through the audience, which spontaneously broke out into song. The popular ditty attested to the villagers' support for Iroko, whatever the case:

"Iroko, Iroko, Iroko, we'll follow.
If he's going, if he's coming,
Iroko we'll follow."

It was an eye-opening spectacle for Osita. He needed no second telling to adapt his campaign. His Igbo got better with each delivery until he was nearly as fluent as the Great Iroko. He certainly became as glib as his opponent, ditching his statistics in favour of fantastical promises and rabble-rousing.

"A great man once said," Patrick told him, in reference to Iroko's manner of speech, "that proverbs are the palm oil by which words are consumed among our people." Osita forced himself to become adept at speaking in parable, a practice he previously derided as "uncivilised." He sat for several nights learning proverbs under his father's tutelage. He reserved a few choice ones for the Great Iroko, mocking his opponent's vulgarity and celebrating Osita's refinement by contrast.

"When a man (like my opponent) does not know where he is going, any road will do. Do we choose someone to send on an errand because he can drink *kai-kai*? No, we choose him because he knows something. We cannot live beside the river and be washing our hands in spit. A vulture is a vulture—no matter how high it flies, it will never become an eagle. Even the biggest Iroko is nothing but chaff when it encounters a determined axe."

Osita was bent on showing off his superior education. Wiser now, he sought to do it in a way that would not alienate his audience. He began to end his speeches with a pithy assertion.

"It was those that spoke Latin, the language of *ukochukwu*—God's missionaries—who said '*Aluta Continua, Victoria Acerta*' which means that our struggle continues but victory is sure. So I greet you all: Aluta Continua!"

The villagers quickly picked up on the refrain "Victoria Acerta," all the while loving the subtle reminder that while the candidate spoke otherwise inaccessible idiom, he possessed a learning and sophistication beyond their fathom. Osita was, therefore, a worthy ambassador—the type of person that Adimora could point outsiders to and proclaim, "We have somebody."

Osita's popularity rose. The marketplaces and motor parks became animated with discussion of the prospects for a *dokinta* chairman. Inebriated patrons of beer parlours acknowledged one another with cries of "Alootah Container." On school playgrounds, children sang the campaign anthem, "Call Him Doctor, He Will Answer," that Patrick had cannily composed to the tune of a church hymn.

News filtered that a surprised Great Iroko was getting increasingly agitated. And desperate. It was Patrick again who advised Osita to do the needful.

"Chair, you know it is only a tree that will stand still while it is about to be cut down; trust me, your opponent is not a tree despite his name of acclaim."

"What do you mean?" Osita queried.

"My chairman, sir, our land is not the white man's land. Here the spirits of the land are still enormously powerful. Your opponent will be making all sorts of charms now to cripple or even kill you. You have to protect yourself."

Osita was steadfast in his refusal to consult the *dibia* that Patrick recommended. Instead, he opted for a Pentecostal preacher. Kachi Madu had grown up with Osita, but since taking to the ministry had become known only as Prophet Holy Thunder Fireman. Osita had laughed when he first heard what he considered a ludicrous name but found the laugh was on him as his former classmate soon garnered the biggest flock for miles. As his ministry had prospered, so had Fireman; his fleet of exotic cars was now surpassed only by those of Cleanout and, of course, Chief Onwuka.

Prophet Fireman embraced Osita in front of the congregation on the appointed Sunday. After Osita had "sown a seed" by making a sizeable cash offering, as commanded by Fireman, the effervescent preacher proceeded to pray for the candidate in typical fire-and-brimstone style. The prayer ended with an anointing during which Fireman placed his hand on Osita's forehead and spoke in tongues.

Osita was familiar with the procedure: the power of the anointing was supposed to literally *fell* him. He did not feel the expected spiritual propulsion as Fireman continued unintelligibly, but he obligingly fell backwards anyway. It would not look good if it appeared that any malevolent spirits attending him, perhaps even foisted upon him by his opponent, were so powerful that they prevented him from receiving Fireman's anointing.

Whether it was the efficacy of Fireman's prayers or sheer adrenaline, Osita found that he bore the demands of the campaign rather well. Usually, whenever he kept a series of late nights or did not eat well, he would come down with malaria or, depending on who was diagnosing the feverish symptoms, typhoid. Now, his days did not end before midnight and began before the sun rose. There was always a meeting to attend or someone or group to endear his campaign to. Sometimes he ate too much; sometimes he didn't eat at all. But he kept well, and whatever supernatural forces the Great Iroko might have tried to unleash did not have any visible effect.

As his campaign gathered steam and popular acclaim grew, Osita received donations from far and wide. On the eve of the PDP primaries, he found he was running a surplus. By all accounts, it was still going to be close between him and the Great Iroko. Patrick advised him that when elections were tight like that, Chief Onwuka usually swung things the way of the candidate that most impressed him.

Patrick was out in the field, supervising last-minute

things, when Osita had a brain wave. He would curry Chief Onwuka's favour by proving conclusively that he was going to be an honest chairman. Without telling Patrick, he called on Onwuka and tendered one million naira, explaining that it was change from the seed money that Onwuka had given him.

"The big masquerade of Adimora. The leopard that watches over the community. The chief that is greater than his peers. You are praised at home, you are praised abroad and you are praised all over the world. As God has blessed you, so have you dispensed blessings to the poor. Our people say that one spoon of soup in a time of need is more valuable than the whole pot when there is abundance. You fed me a big spoon when I was in famine. I will, however, not be like the man who choked because he took another mouthful before swallowing what was already in his mouth. They say that if you want to know the end, you should look at the beginning. Anyone who can steal an egg will steal the poultry. As God is my witness, Doctor Osita Anumba is incapable of stealing an ant."

Chief Onwuka looked at Osita in disbelief and then burst out laughing before grasping him in a bear hug.

"Dokinta, I have not asking you for change? This money is your money. If Chief Onwuka are needing money, it is not this kind of money I am need. Keep it, my son. I know you are try to show honest but keep it. Alootah must container even if Victoria echetram."

Election Day went well. The party delegates from all the wards formed orderly queues and voted from noon at the Amaoye primary school which the party had chosen as voting center. The voting was not only for chairmanship candidates. Delegates also voted for councillors. There were twelve councillor positions, and several candidates had made the cut to contest each nomination. Voting was long, ending after sundown.

The PDP had only a ramshackle office in the local government area. The last time the party tried to use it for vote collation, a disgruntled candidate had thrust the legs of a chair into the rotating ceiling fan. The machine-gun sound that resulted had sent everyone scampering for cover. In the confusion, the candidate grabbed the filled results sheets and started eating them. When order was eventually restored and he was rounded on, all he could say for himself was, "Water, please."

A more secure and spacious place was needed today. The ballots were therefore escorted to Chief Onwuka's residence which was under heavy guard. Only party bigwigs, sundry men of influence and the chairman candidates were admitted into the expansive compound. The various retinues and curious onlookers were kept outside under inadequate canopies erected in the dusty field opposite Onwuka's gates. A raucous atmosphere developed, continuing through the night as food and drink were served and political songs sung.

Everyone knew that this was when the real primaries started. And ended. Some European potentate of antiquity had said that it was not those who cast votes but those who counted them that mattered. But that was because he had not been here before.

Here, it was those who decided what had been counted that mattered. Whatever the ballots said, in the end, it would come down to a list agreed upon after intense horse-trading by the local movers and shakers, now sequestered inside the house of the biggest one of them.

The whole process up until now had been a charade—but an inescapable one. The electioneering had to be done even though everyone knew how the results would be decided. Not to go through the mill of campaigning and lobbying would be to have disrespected the people, an abomination fatal to even the best candidate.

Besides, the exercise was one of those things that spread money around and enabled subsistence for many. Money was given and received at every turn. It was "settlement," the only dividend of democracy that was available to most. Patrick, astute as ever, knew he had to break it down to a candidate still brimming with idealism.

"My chair, you see the party officials who screen the candidates? We must settle them. Anybody who is somebody in this process, we must settle. We cannot miss out even one person; otherwise, it can be like the one finger that is dipped in palm oil which ended up staining the whole hand. Ward leaders? Settle. Women leaders? Youth leaders? Anybody called 'leader' in the party? Settle. The people who organise rallies? Them too. And of course those who attend the rallies."

"Huh?" Osita interjected. Patrick continued without missing a beat.

"Don't look so surprised, my chair—yes, even those that attend rallies except you want to be talking to empty space. As for the delegates who will vote at the primaries, once they are known, ah, their own settlement will be special. You see, they didn't spend all that money settling those who determined they would be delegates just to come and be looking at candidates' faces o. So you must fill their hearts with enough joy, by putting something they can touch in their hands, to make them cast their votes for you."

Most of the settlement money came from the candidates and their supporters. Patrick took care of the settling on behalf of Osita, who salved his conscience by convincing himself that the disbursements continually recounted by Patrick were merely "campaign costs." Yet all this was just to qualify one to be in the frame for the final list that would be decided tonight and announced as the results of the primaries.

Chief Onwuka's compound had several mansions. He had dedicated one to the day's proceedings. Osita and the Great Iroko were part of it at first, each jostling to get his preferred candidates for councilor put on the list. Both men knew, the Great Iroko from experience and Osita from being tutored by Patrick on the dynamics, that it was dangerous to win the seat without having your loyalists dominate the council. A simple impeachment motion at the council's first meeting would abruptly end the chairman's tenure if the councilors were not his men.

Eventually, Osita and the Great Iroko were banished to a plush anteroom so that the negotiations on the chairmanship candidate could begin. The Great Iroko had waited out this process many times before, albeit outside the compound. He promptly stretched out on the sofa and fell asleep.

Osita was nervous but, given his opponent's countenance, was determined not to show it. He feigned disinterest even as his stomach churned. He wished Patrick were with him, but his trusted aide had not been deemed high enough in the hierarchy to merit admission. As the hours passed, his edginess waned, giving way to fatigue. Yet, he could not sleep. By 3:00 a.m., he was in envy and awe of the Great Iroko, who had stirred only once to go to the bathroom before resuming the snoring.

And then suddenly it was over.

The door to the room opened, and Chief Onwuka's bald pate appeared. Osita could not help but notice that he looked remarkably alert for that time of the morning. The Great Iroko woke with a start, as if on cue. Before he could gather himself, Chief Onwuka curtly told him, "Iroko, I want to talking to my chairman. You are wait here for me, are you understanding me? You are not go anywhere. I will coming back, now-now, to talking to you."

Osita did not believe what he was hearing. The Great Iroko's countenance fell and he seemed to reduce in size. Osita's heart was now pounding. He could hardly breathe.

Chief Onwuka gave him an expansive smile and said, "*Dokinta*, my chair, please come outside with me."

As Osita stepped out of the room and closed the door on a crestfallen Great Iroko, Chief Onwuka composed himself. It had been a close election, but the *dokinta* had shaded it on the votes cast. Onwuka was astonished at how well the neophyte had done. Onwuka had made a note to assimilate Patrick, the organiser, into his personal staff. "This children have really impress me," he had said over and over as the votes were tallied.

There was only one problem—anyone who accounted honestly for money given to him for campaigns would similarly account for local government money. That would not do, and *dokinta* would have to learn. Onwuka had therefore decided to put the Great Iroko on the list as the PDP's chairmanship candidate for the Adimora local government council.

Peter Chika, based in Houston, has won numerous international writing awards, including special merit in the Amex Bank Review Awards and a bronze in the Shell-Economist Prize. Among his six academic degrees, he cherishes his MSc from Oxford and PhD from Oxford the most.

In his spare time, Peter writes short stories wherever inspiration strikes—on planes, in cafes, or anywhere he can. His work has appeared in anthologies like *Tunnel of Lost Stories*.

He's the author of the bestselling short story collection, *The Condom and Other Stories*.

Black and Blue

Winnie Enunosowo Eka-Williams

Saturdays were the only days I could rest, life as a lawyer fresh out of law school was as hectic as it could get, from competing with other lawyers in the firm I worked for a sitting at the grown-up's table to trying to balance work life with social life, Saturdays were created for me to take time for myself and do what I enjoy and that was why I found myself in a bookstore every Saturday looking through various books and trying to decide which I was going to read, I was a regular at the bookstore, I knew all the workers and the security man always cajoled me to give him *something* every time I visited.

The Saturday I met Michael, I was wearing a blue chiffon top, my favourite everyday black jeans and brown leather slippers with my tote bag. It was a rainy day, and I was thankful I was already inside the store before the clouds gathered; I had forgotten my glasses, and I thought it was a bad omen because who forgets their glasses when they're going to a bookstore?

The store was quiet; some people were on their laptops in the lounge area, and some were at the cafe helping their selves to a cup of coffee, I didn't have a particular book on my mind, so I was glancing through and reading the synopsis and just judging them by their covers as I always do. I could never buy a book whose cover wasn't aesthetically pleasing to my eye. I had picked up a novel when the door opened, and there he was; he stood there in his 6 inches glory, with a full face of beard and gold-rimmed glasses, the scent of the whole store changed, and his strong, musky scent filled the space, he smelt like fresh wood and clean glass-very distinct description, I know.

I quickly looked back into my book and continued to read. I felt his presence as he moved around the store, his head showing at the top of every shelf of the row he walked due to his height. I had read the synopsis of the book I was holding at least three times without remembering to understand what I was reading. I walked around more, took another book and turned my back; it was a good story. I had finally found the book to get when I heard it.

"He dies at the end. And she goes off with her first love."

I whipped my head so fast I was pretty sure I must've cracked a bone; the book fell out of my hand. We bent together to pick it up, and we bumped into each other. This was so cliché, I was embarrassed at myself; he picked up the book while I held my forehead and got up slowly; we stared at each other, then burst out in laughter.

"I'm so sorry," he finally said when he had stopped laughing, adjusted himself and looked at me.

"For breaking my head or spoiling my book?" I asked.

He offered to pay for my book, but I refused, so he asked if he could get me a cup of coffee. I obliged, we sat opposite each other beside the large window while we waited for our coffee, and I began to read the book I had paid for. At the same time, he just looked at me, I could feel his eyes on my face, but I resisted the urge to look back at him and pretended to be completely indulged in my book. However, I just could not take it, I set my book down calmly and looked at him.

"Did the bump leave a scar on my face?" I asked

"What? Oh no, there's nothing on your face apart from beauty," he replied and showed off his perfect set of white teeth.

I rolled my eyes and smiled a little. "Okay, good because I'm a lawyer, and I can sue you."

"Oh really? Wow!" We would not want that; I have actually been looking for a good law firm to handle my company's legal needs. Do you work at anyone?'

"Yes – I'm a junior associate for Asuquo & Asuquo."

"I've heard about them; they were on my list, actually. If I employ the services of your firm promise me you won't sue me?"

"I promise," I giggled and took a sip of my coffee. People really do find love in the strangest places. I entered my house, and my mom was seated watching *Zee World*, she watched nothing else and knew all the Indian songs they played, she glanced at me.

"Madam, namaste." I held back my laughter. "Good evening, Mommy." I handed the bag of bananas and groundnuts I bought for her

"Every time you'll be bringing fruits, when will you bring your husband, Anne?" I knew where this conversation was going, and I rolled my eyes.

"You'll be thirty this year and still no sign of boyfriend, talk less of a man that will marry you."

She went on and on while taking breaks to munch on the bananas I brought for her. She went on and on, and I just sat there looking at her. I didn't blame her; she wanted to see her daughter married like any other mother. I have two sisters, and they're both married despite my being the first girl. Law school was hard; I did not have any time for myself, speaking even more for another person, and I never really found the one. When I told the men who approached me that I was keeping myself for marriage, they'd always responded that they knew my type and tried to persuade me against my better judgment.

The only boy I had dated was in NYSC; his name was Timi, and I was so sure that he was going to propose to me when we returned home, and he invited me to dinner. Apparently, he wanted to break up with me because he just gotten married the previous Saturday. From then on, I did not bother anymore; I went about my life and only experienced love in the fake scenarios I created in my head and the happy-ever-afters I read in novels; that was enough romance for me.

I could not sleep. Michael had dropped me off in front of my house and did not bother asking for my number, and I could not stop thinking about what the reason might be; I decided to push the thought and just go to bed.

***

The weekend went by in a flash; the much-dreaded Monday had come, and I had a case in court, which was a very stressful process. I returned to the office past three, almost closing time, and I had to report to my principal, Mr Okafor, before going home. I knocked on his door and dragged my skirt further down before opening it.

Mr Okafor was a weird man; his eyes always lingered in places they were not needed, and his hands liked to follow suit. I always left his door wide open when I was in his office and tried to keep a safe distance. I walked in, and immediately, it hit me – I knew this scent from somewhere; the man sitting opposite Mr Okafor turned, and there he was - it was Michael; he gave me a small smile.

"Oh, Miss Anne, I was just about to send for you. How did it go in court today?'

"It was fine, sir. The case was adjourned to next month."

He nodded.

"This is Mr. Michael Orji; he is the CEO of MO Breweries, and he is our newest client - he said he wants you to personally handle all the legal matters of his company." I was beyond shocked; this was a big elevation from my position as a junior associate. I had to contain my joy. I smiled and thanked him. he offered to drive me home, and I agreed

"I'm sorry if I put you on the spot." He opened the passenger seat, and I got in before he went round to the driver's

"It is really fine. If anything, I'm very excited and grateful to you."

We spoke about our jobs and the company, and what I was required to do; he mentioned that they had an annual award ceremony and he would really like for me to come.

I wanted to, but it was a Sunday, and I absolutely dreaded leaving my room on Sundays, I did church online for a reason, I said I was going to think about it, and he accepted, we got to my house, and I dropped out, he still had not asked for my number, and that made me sad, but I pushed it aside and thanked him before stepping out of his car.

My phone beeped immediately after I got out of the bathroom after showering; I dived on my bed to get it expecting a message from Michael; I was so pissed when I saw that it was a message from Airtel; I threw the phone back on the bed, what was I even thinking? he did not ask for my number after meeting me again. I really hated mixed signals. Maybe he was leaning towards friends? but friends have each other's numbers; even enemies have each other's numbers, so what exactly was going on?

I went on Instagram and searched his full name, and lots of Michael Orji's popped out; I put on my FBI cap and started eliminating them until I found the one.

Bingo. There it was; he had over a thousand followers and fifty posts, and I had like two hundred followers; I went through his page from vacations in

Dubai, Miami and America to business meetings and the gym; his whole life was displayed on his page.

I took my time going through the pictures and reading the comments; I noticed he didn't post anyone apart from himself. There was a particular picture that attracted my eye; he was in an army green shirt with a white beach shirt. I smiled to myself and double-tapped.

I double-tapped?

I threw my phone and picked it up again; I liked a picture from 2019 in 2022. I was so embarrassed that I quickly logged out of my Instagram and took it as a sign to go to bed already; I could not stop thinking of how terribly I had disgraced myself and why I was thinking about him so much.

★★★

My dress was rather tight today, but it was the only thing that did not need ironing. Plus, it was a Friday, so I did not put much thought into it when I wore it. I got to work and settled in, then took the proceedings to the principal; I adjusted my dress to the longest it could be, which was below my knees, before stepping into his office.

I was secretly hoping to see you know who sitting just like he was the other day but his office revealed only Mr Okafor sitting on his chair with his preluding belly, cucumber in one hand, groundnut on the other, sweating profusely amidst the air conditioner blowing In his office, he eyed me when I walked in and continued to rock his chair.

"Ani-baby."

"I had told him many times that I thought that nickname was rather inappropriate, but he continuously ignored me."

"Sir, you asked for me?"

"Hm." His eyes moved from my face and landed on my cleavage. "You are adding o."

I ignored the comment and shifted uncomfortably on my feet.

"Come over here and take the invitation for the award event for Mr Michael Orji's company. We have to represent, and he specially asked for you," he sighed at the last part.

I moved slowly to him, and he turned his chair. I moved across the table and kept a safe distance before stretching my hand for the envelope. He stretched his hand, and when I held the envelope, he dragged me to his lap and held me close. I was surely feeling what I was not supposed to feel. I tried to wriggle away, but that just seemed to be pleasing him

"You think I don't see what you do, putting on such a dress to tempt me."

He smelled like the mixture of sweat in a busy market afternoon.

"I am a man o and I am not blind."

I stomped on his leg with my heels, and he let me go. Considering how hard it is to get a job in Nigeria, I had to hold my tongue, I had complained bitterly about Mr Okafor and what he did to junior associates, but the female senior associates said it was the only chance to have a sit on the table, if this was the only chance, then I did not want to sit at the table.

"Sir, this is completely inappropriate. The next time it happens, I will not take it lightly."

I left his office knowing the punishment that awaited me was going to be lots of unnecessary paperwork and errands. I tried to push what had happened and calm my anger, so I opened the invitation card.

I really hope you'll be able to come
P.S Wear something red
M.

I was grinning from ear to ear, I read the short message over and over, registering his handwriting in my head, it was neat and slanty with a particular curve to it, I quickly put away the letter when I saw Jewel working towards me, he was the office's gossip, and I surely did not want to hear about his plans for the weekend or the people he caught kissing in the coffee room.

"Ah, Anne, this dress is the bomb. Is it for your new client?"

I feigned ignorance and looked everywhere else but at his face.

"Ah, the walls have ears, you know; I saw when Michael Orji walked into this office, asking everyone for Anne, and I heard that he specifically asked you to handle his company's affairs," he finished with a satisfied grin on his face, his hand in his waist.

"I see," was all I said before I excused myself, smiling all the way to the bathroom.

He asked everyone about me?

Still smiling to myself.

***

It was eight-thirty, and I still had not found a decent dress to wear for the award ceremony. My hair was in a high ponytail, and I kept my makeup minimal and classy, as a lawyer, I hardly had any bright clothes - my clothes are mostly black, white, navy blue or ash so wearing something 'red' was definitely a challenge, it was already too late to buy one, and I was running out of options.

I remembered I had sisters, and I quickly called Sarah. I remember the dress she wore for her engagement party. It was a red tightly fitted dress with a square neck and a high slit. I rushed to her house and picked it up; her husband was away - he was a pilot and was barely at home. I slipped on the dress, carried my clutch and bathed myself in her *Elizabeth Arden* perfume. She made me promise to give her the full gist before I ran out the door; I was already late, such a terrible impression.

The place was hard to find; we had taken a wrong turn, and the driver kept asking me for the location even after I told him to use his map. I stepped out of the car and into the building. I handed my invitation card to the bouncer, and an usher asked me to follow, the place was dimly lit apart from the stage, which was the obvious centre of attraction that held all the light, we passed through the tables, and she kept going until we were up the stairs and in a private bar with VVIP written on the table.

I was going to tap her and tell her she had misunderstood, but when we got there, she showed another bouncer my invitation, and he confirmed it on the list and let me in. The booth was a twelve-seater; six men were already seated with two other ladies.

I said 'hi' and took my seat uncomfortably, no sign of Michael. The ceremony was going on, and people were talking and mingling, I opened my bag, took out my phone, went to my books app and started reading my ebook, my number one rule was never go to a social event without a book, I was emersed in my book, and I kept flipping pages after pages that I didn't realise someone was watching me

"Sorry to interrupt, I'm Kehinde Coker." He stretched his hand to me.

I put my phone away and sat up. "Nice to meet you, Anne Uchenna."

"Oh, I see you met Kehinde."

I know that scent. I turned around; he was wearing a black suit with a bright red tie. Red was not the dress code, as everyone else was dressed in other colours; I got up and shook his hand.

"I'm happy you could make it." He gave a small smile, and he still held my hands; Kehinde coughed, and Michael sat beside me and turned to the rest of the group.

"Guys, meet Anne," he introduced me and introduced them to me. They were all friends from university, and they all had their businesses and were here to support him, some even flew all the way from America, as in Kehinde's case, to support him.

"Oh, you're *the* Anne," one of his friends, I believe his name was Derek added, after I was introduced. I did not know what *the* Anne meant, so I just gave a puzzled look.

"Oh, Michael has not been able to shut up about the girl he met at the bookstore."

I was blushing so hard; my heart was performing a whole gymnastic routine, but I managed to conceal it and give a small smile.

"Okay, that is enough."

It was Michael scratching the back of his head and smiling at me. He got up to get me something to drink, and I continued the conversation with the rest of them and Kehinde. The night was slow but fun; I was on my third cup of Chapman. I told them I did not drink, and no one seemed to have a problem with it. Michael was busy, so Kehinde just kept me company.

I was finally exhausted; Michael's company had won five awards, and everyone seemed to love him as their cheer got louder each time he came for his award. I excused myself and said goodbye to everyone. They wouldn't let me go, but I explained I was having a headache and really needed to leave.

Kehinde offered to drop me off, but I declined, saying I didn't want him to miss the party because of me, I looked round for Michael, but I couldn't find him so I gave up and stood outside the hotel while I waited for my ride, it was freezing and I had to hug my arms while standing outside, I felt the heavy material on my shoulders and I turned to see Michael smiling at me

"I'm sorry, it is a madhouse in there. I didn't realise you left already."

"Oh no, it's completely fine. I had lots of fun; thank you for inviting me again." He was looking at me with a sad smile. He fastened the suit on me properly

"I was hoping I would get to spend some time with you tonight. You look absolutely stunning."

"Thank you, I like your tie."

I smiled at him.

"I guess you figured out red was not the dress code, and I wanted you to match with me; I'm not sorry for it, though." I smiled; my heart was in a rage, and my knees really were weak.

"Truth is- ever since I saw you at that bookstore, I haven't been able to stop thinking about you, Anne. I was going to take things slowly, but I didn't want to waste your time. My knees were going to give way, and I hoped to fall into his arms; I looked everywhere but his face and when I did, I was lost in those eyes.

"You don't have to say anything. I just wanted to express how I felt – "

"I feel the same way," I blurted. Oh, where had my dignity gone? I was supposed to say I'll think about it so I don't seem easy to have. I looked away, and he smiled.

"It is really cold. Let me drop you at home."

I nodded.

★★★

August 5, 2022. I dragged myself out of bed, got ready for work and got out of my room

"He has not proposed?" my mother asked as she scanned my fingers. I folded them and moved to the table

"You owe me ten thousand." My mother turned to my sister, who was visiting, and scoffed, "I told you he wouldn't do it before she turned thirty."

My sister frowned and rolled her eyes. My love life had become a bet; I shook my head and started eating, 'Happy birthday to me'.

The office was even busier, from client to client, and with multiple briefs, I was drowning in the work I had to do when my phone beeped.

Happy birthday, babe. Dinner at my place?

I smiled at the text. Michael and I had been dating for seven months now, and for my birthday, he sent me flowers for a week leading to my birthday. My mom complained that there were no other spaces to keep them, and we wanted a ring, not vegetables; I ignored her and arranged them neatly in my room. This will be the day; I could feel it.

I went to the principal by past three to submit my last files before I grabbed my bag and ran to the nail salon. I refused to be proposed to with my nails looking undone, just in case. I got them done, bought a new dress and went home. By eight-thirty, I was done with my makeup; I slipped on the gold silk dress and stepped out of my room to total darkness; I moved for the light switch to put it on.

"SURPRISE!"

I shifted back and held my chest; I was so scared. I scanned through the room: my sisters and their husbands, her kids, my mother, Michael and Kehinde, with other people I was not so sure I knew, but I was entirely happy; Michael moved forward and hugged me.

"Happy birthday, babe! Will you make me the happiest man in the world and marry me?" He got on his knees and brought out the ring. I was going to cry, but this makeup took hours, and I didn't want to ruin it because of the pictures after; I held them back and nodded frantically.

"Yes, of course. I'll marry you, babe."

We kissed, and the room roared with claps, champagne popping and merriment - my life was a movie.

Our wedding was held in December, and Michael wanted it to be in South Africa, so that was where the white wedding was held while the traditional marriage was in my home town; we had moved into a new house, and I was still sorting out the last of my things at home.

"No matter what, he is your husband; the two have become one. Know that you do not have any room in this house," my mother kept ringing it every time I spoke to her about an argument Michael and I had.

One time, she said I should stop talking to outsiders about my marriage when I was talking to her, my mother. When did the woman that gave birth to me become an outsider? I stopped talking to her about our arguments. The first time we had an argument was when I had just got back from work. he had not gone to work that day, and I had been in court all day. I rushed upstairs, got changed and microwaved the stew while I boiled rice before serving it to him.

"Is this today's stew?" he asked after making a funny face at the stew. I had made the stew with other soups the day after our wedding, since my office was not willing to give me a break. I had to resume immediately after the wedding, and the work was dumped full force on me as a wedding gift.

"I made it yesterday, but I microwaved it," I replied and got up to taste his stew.

'I do not eat microwaved food, all my meals must be made from scratch" I looked at him in disbelief, when did this start? I microwaved his food for him all the time when we were dating. How did he expect me to make food every day before and after work?

"Oh, that's almost impossible due to my work schedule. I can reheat the stew if you – " His hand came crashing on my face. Between the pain and the fact he actually slapped me, I couldn't say which one hurt more. I shifted back and held the edge of the table. he stomped off to the room and locked the door.

The couch was so uncomfortable, and the mosquitoes fed off my skin all night. The next morning, he got dressed, left his breakfast, which was freshly made, untouched and left. I quickly dressed up and used my powder to cover the red mark that was on my face. I sat on my table in deep thought. I had always said that the last thing I would let a man do was to hit me, and there I was, completely lost and confused when the delivery man brought a bunch of roses and delivered them to me.

"Sorry, babe," was all it read.

Who did I marry?

The next months helped me to answer this question. I got kicked in the stomach and broke a rib for staining our bed when I was on my period but he sent a huge teddy bear, I was stepped on numerous times when I did not pick up his calls because I was in court, he got me a new car and he twisted my fingers when I asked him why he did not wear his wedding ring anymore, he got me Gucci shoes.

Our one-year anniversary came, and I kept telling myself every day, 'I'm going to leave, I will leave,' but I never did. I could not look at myself in the mirror, such a weak and utterly useless person. I found out I was pregnant three weeks ago, and I had kept it to myself. I told my mom about the abuse first.

"Anita, time is not on your side. There is no need to be sentimental. You don't have a room in this house o, hm," was all she told me.

I went back home that day. I held my stomach and decided I was going to tell him; this baby was going to change our lives.

After cooking ogbono soup from scratch as he requested and pounding his yam, I served him that evening

"I'm pregnant." I smiled at him when I sat beside him after serving him.

"With whose permission?" He looked up at me with a cross face.

I struggled to understand the question. Did I need someone's permission to be pregnant with his child?

"Whose permission?"

He slammed the table and sent the plates and my three hours of hard labour crashing down.

"I am not ready for a child, get rid of it and make me something else to eat." He got up and left the table.

I followed him into the room.

"What do you mean get rid of it Michael? It is our baby and I am definitely not getting rid of it." I stood my ground; enough is enough. This baby was very important for me, why would I abort my baby?

"Fine, then I'll do it for you." And he did.

I saw black and blue when the impact of the kicks reached my belly. I held the bed and struggled to stand up when the stool for the vanity table was destroyed on my back, making me fall again. black and blue was all I saw, sweat, tears and blood flowing from my body.

I looked up and saw the man I married; the tears refused to flow. When he stopped and took his car keys, I heard his car drive out. I silently prayed. God was a distant figure to me; I never considered Him, but this particular time, I prayed to Him for anything and for nothing. I slowly got up and asked our security to take me to the hospital.

"We really do not know how, but the baby is safe. Considering the injuries you sustained, it is almost impossible for the baby to still be alive."

I closed my eyes in tears, and I deeply thanked God, and I made a vow to Him to serve him the rest of my days and in that moment. I felt a rush in my spirit, and peace suddenly overwhelmed me, and a voice said:

"Anastasia."

I wanted to correct it and say I was Anne, but I did not.

After two weeks, I was discharged, and I headed straight for the police station. The case dragged on for months and caused an uproar on *Twitter*, with comments about how I was only in it out of desperation, and I was after his money, but I held on. He had connections, but I had a higher force; he was found guilty, and eight months later, I had Anastasia.

"What does this name even mean?" my mother asked.

"Rebirth."

Winnie Enunosowo Eka-Williams, a law graduate and poet who hails from Cross River State, Nigeria. A passionate reader and writer, she began crafting stories at the age of twelve, finding it a powerful outlet for her creativity.

Now residing in Abuja, she dedicates her time to her studies and writing while occasionally engaging in public speaking.

Heartbeats & Blueprints

Zainab O. Bankole

Mo's morning started like every other day, stepping into the chaos and smell of the hospital where she worked. But there was something different about this morning, and Mo knew it had everything to do with the email she had received the night before, the one she had been waiting for nearly three years. The light smile on her face turned into a grimace as she walked into the hospital. If there was anything she hated about being a nurse aside from the less-than-satisfying pay, it was the noxious blend of antiseptic, sweat, and *Izal* that clung to the faded walls of the hospital.

Sometimes, she wondered if the woman who did the cleaning could use something other than *Izal*, the unmistakable stench never did anything to improve her day every morning she walked in through the entrance. The fluorescent lights overhead shined brightly, giving her a good view of the overcrowded waiting area. Patients spilt out of every available space, some sitting straight in attention as if waiting to be called into the doctor's office any second, others slumped in their seats, their faces etched with pain and fatigue. She knew some of them would have been there since four a.m. in the morning, hoping to see the doctor before the day ended.

She sighed, as she arrived at the area she shared with the other nurses, "Good morning, Nurse Mo." The cleaner, Folusho, who was mopping the nurses' station acknowledged her.

She gave the young lady a small smile. "Good morning. How are you doing?"

"I am fine ooh. Nurse Titi just left, she said she couldn't wait for you to arrive because she has an event to attend today," Folusho informed her.

"Yes, I noticed she already signed out, thank you." She didn't bother asking about Yewande and Dunni who were supposed to do the day shift with her, they never resumed until about fifty minutes to an hour after resumption time.

She took a deep breath, to prepare herself for the long battle ahead before heading to the wards. Every day was a fight for survival, not just for the patients, but for the staff as well. If it wasn't the lack of medical supplies, it was the broken equipment or the endless stream of patients that far outnumbered the available beds and medical personnel. She couldn't wait to be out of this environment which was dampening her potential, and after the mail she had received from the U.S. hospital to schedule a final interview last night, Mo knew it was only a matter of time before she would be out of Nigeria.

"Good morning, Nurse Mo!" Dr Adeoye called out as she walked into Ward 3, He was doing his final rounds; his voice was strained with the weariness that came from another night spent battling the impossible.

"Good morning, Doctor," she replied, hands behind her.

"Please attend to the patients in beds 3 and 5. I updated their charts earlier. I can't find Nurse Titi. She's probably left."

"Alright," she moved in the direction of the beds.

"Also, check on the patient on bed 6, ward 6. His blood pressure was very high yesterday; I told Nurse Ola to administer hydrochlorothiazide to stabilize him, but he needs to be constantly monitored."

"Okay doctor, I will check on him." She said, leaving him to his rounds.

***

By early mid-afternoon, Mo was running on fumes, her leg aching from the constant movement, but with no end in sight. Mo had finally gotten a few minutes to rest her feet and was eating her bland lunch which was two pieces of doughnuts she had bought from one of the mini shops in the hospital and a bottle of Viju milk drink when Folusho ran into the nurse station breathing heavily and managed to let out

"Nurse Mo, Doctor Atinuke said I should call you. They just brought in a car accident patient, she is in the emergency room."

Mo jumped up and hurried to the emergency room; it wasn't too hard to locate the new patient she had been summoned for; a young man lay on bed 2, his body covered in cuts, and blood flowed from a big gash on his arm.

"A car accident victim losing blood. We need to stabilize him before we can do surgery." Dr Atinuke explained in clipped tones.

"Okay," Mo said, slipping into her professional mode, the only way she knew how to cope with the endless suffering around her.

"His pulse is weak, and his blood pressure is dropping," Dr Atinuke said, her hands moving quickly as she adjusted the IV drip. "We're losing him." Mo moved to the patient's side, her trained eyes assessing his condition. Despite the blood and the trauma, there was something about him that stood out. His face, though bruised and battered, held an unusual calm, almost as if he was at peace with whatever fate awaited him. She shook her head to get rid of her thoughts; this wasn't the time for sentiments.

"Hang in there," she muttered as she adjusted the oxygen mask over his nose and mouth.

★★★

Mo let out a sigh of relief as they wheeled the patient out to surgery after a tense hour of working in silence to stabilize him. And when she walked out of the surgery room nearly three hours later, her feet were numb, her mind was exhausted, and she was ready to call it a day. Thankfully, the internal bleeding hadn't been as severe as she had feared. Mo couldn't place her hands on it, but she had a hunch throughout the surgery that the patient would survive because the man, whoever he was, seemed to have the will to live.

She dragged her feet back to the nurse's station, passing the waiting area still lined with several patients, their eyes trailing after her with a mixture of hope and desperation. Arriving at the station, she trashed her half-eaten exposed doughnuts and placed the halfway-consumed beverage in her bag, with plans to refrigerate it when she got home before collapsing on one of the chairs, giving herself a moment of rest.

"*Pele.*" Dunni threw her a sympathetic smile.

"Thank you. I am surprised you are still here."

Dunni laughed. "Haba nah, is that how bad I am?" She checked the collar of her polo shirt and then tucked the part of her uniform peeking out of her tote bag. "Anyways, my husband is running late, but he will be here soon."

"I thought as much," she nodded with a slight smile on her face. Dunni never left late, and it was already almost fifteen minutes past six.

Yewande walked in then, her face set in a frown that communicated to anyone who cared that she was ready to close for the day.

"Madam, why you spoil face like this?" Dunni asked playfully.

"Omo, I am just tired. All these people are just overworking somebody, and it is not like they are paying someone well," Yewande complained.

"I tell you ooh. Person just dey do mumu work." Dunni replied.

"I am so tired. It is like I am going to start my UK processing again," Yewande said before passing Mo an ID card.

"What is this?" she asked, turning the card in her hand and catching a glimpse of the name *Tejumola Adeyemi*.

Yewande glanced up from her bag, giving Mo a look she knew only meant she needed a favour from her.

"Tunde gave it to me on my way, and he said it

belongs to the emergency patient. Please help me put it in his bedside cabinet. I have to leave now, or I won't be able to beat that traffic at Ojo."

She frowned. "You can just drop it on your way nah, how many minutes is that going to take you?" she asked, sitting up, with narrowed eyes and lips pressed in a thin, tight line.

"Mo, please," Yewande pleaded, already shrugging off her uniform. "They have moved him to Ward 8. I can't go all the way there. Abeg."

"Okay, no wahala," she sighed in defeat a while later.

"Thank you." Yewande smiled, picked up her bag, and added, "Goodnight."

Dunni picked up her bags too, "Let's leave together, my husband is already downstairs." She said, placing the handle of her big tote bag that seemed to contain everything one might ever need, including an emergency change of clothes and underwear, on her shoulder.

"Okay, that's good. I would follow you halfway then." Yewande said with a bright smile on her face.

"Goodnight Mo," they said.

She watched them leave and felt her life bland in comparison to theirs. They walked briskly like they were eager to get home and move on to the next activity of the day as she was sure they were; Dunni, probably to spend time with her husband and prepare the home-cooked meals, snacks, and healthy fruit juices or smoothies, she brought to work every day. Yewande, to prepare to enjoy Lagos nightlife with her friends, like she did most days. Mo would later see the update on her Snapchat status when she woke up to prepare for work the next morning.

She sighed, turning the ID card still in her hands. She glanced at it again and found herself drawn to the warm yet intense eyes of the man in the picture. He was even more stunning with those deep brown eyes she was yet to see. He was smiling at the camera, but his eyes were so focused and aware that it felt like he was looking right into her soul.

She moved her eyes away from his face and focused on the other information on the card.

"Tejumola Adeyemi. Principal Architect at Vertex Architecture."

Mo smiled. Although she didn't know this man or much about architecture, what he did sounded important.

Mo stood up, just as Titi walked in, "Mo, you still dey here?" She seemed genuinely shocked.

"I still dey ooh, good evening." Mo replied good naturedly, glancing at her phone. It was 7:09, which meant she had spent an hour past her working hours.

"Good evening. I am sorry I am late. I finished cooking late because Funke was not feeling well and was being very clingy. When I left, the traffic was already serious. You know it is closing hours." Titi explained.

"No problem," Mo said, biting back the words she really wanted to say. She didn't tell Titi that she always resumed late but left early every day, or that if she left home earlier, she would have made it earlier, or ask her why she always used her kids as an excuse. After all, even Nurse Fifi and Chika, who were supposed to run the shift with her were not yet around at over an hour after their resumption time.

She simply sighed and added the 'terrible work ethics of colleagues' to her mental list of reasons to leave Nigeria as soon as possible.

She picked up her bag with the ID card and bade Titi a good night.

On her way out, Mo passed by Ward 8 to drop the ID card in Tejumola's bedside drawer and watched him for a moment, a strange feeling creeping into her chest.

There was something about him, something that made her want to know more about him. Perhaps it was his confident aura that held a quiet strength and steadiness that made one feel safe, his permanent smile, or how handsome he was even though he was lying in bed in the hospital gown that had been worn for him after the surgery. As she watched him, she wondered if his family had been contacted or if he even had one nearby. Mo checks his IV line one final time before leaving. She had to get home, or she might slump from exhaustion.

***

Mo ditched her flat shoes for her indoor fuzzy slippers as she walked through the door to the apartment. She inhaled the sweet aroma of her home's air freshener; it was a breath of fresh air compared to the smell at the hospital. She dropped her bag on the couch and propped up several throw pillows to support her back before sitting down. She searched through her bag for her phone to catch up on her messages and missed calls.

As usual, most of her messages were from WhatsApp groups she had joined for travelling opportunities and the ones created for updates at work. There were five messages from her brother asking about the best place to take his girlfriend on a date, two from her dad from their conversation the previous day (she had forgotten to respond before going to bed last night, and one from her mum).

"Have you eaten today?" It read.

The message was sent around 2:12 pm, and it was followed by two missed calls. Mo's lips twitched into a smile as she dialled her mother's number; her mother's texts were always a mix of concern and reprimand, as if she couldn't decide if the gentle or firm approach would work best.

"Good evening, mum," Mo said as she picked on the second ring.

"Good evening, my dear. How was work?" She asked.

"It was fine, ma." Mo considered telling her mum about Tejumola but decided against it. Her mum was her closest person on earth after her Dad and brother, but she could already foresee her mum turning the entire thing into a drama. She could almost hear her saying: "What if you were supposed to meet this way? Maybe he's the love of your life that you have been waiting for, like the dramas."

Her mum was a hopeless romantic and will no doubt turn the entire situation into one of her soap operas.

"Okay, that's good. I went to the market in preparation for the group's yearly party today. I was going to send you a video of some of the lace I saw, but I knew you would be at work..."

Mo listened as her mum went on about the yearly party she was hosting for her group of friends at the end of the year. While Mo loved her mother to a fault because she was the closest person she had to a female best friend, she was still her mum, and she constantly worried about her being single at twenty-nine with no end in sight

She was always urging her to go out more, get friends, and mix with people her age, and while Mo wished she could, she had long decided it wasn't her. It was another major reason why she wanted to leave the country; she had long discovered that Nigeria wasn't her kind of space, despite being Nigerian.

The people were always eager to break the rules, there was corruption everywhere, and everyone seemed judgmental yet willing to do absolutely anything, even highly immoral things, to get whatever they wanted. It was so different from the sort of life Mo had always dreamed of.

Mo had always wanted an orderly, fair, and just life. She also dreamed of being in an enabling environment, one that Nigeria doesn't offer, and as much as she loved Nigerian food, the culture, the vibes of the people, the sass, the language, and all the good things that came with the package of being Nigerian, it just doesn't seem like the best place for someone with her personality to thrive.

"I'd send the pictures of the venue's decoration theme the designer sent to me and the pictures of the three laces I couldn't decide on to you on WhatsApp, okay?" Her mum said, breaking through her train of thought.

"Okay, ma," she replied.

"Have you eaten?" she asked

"No, ma. I called you as I got in. As soon as I get off the phone, I will get something to eat," Mo said.

"Okay, go and get something to eat ooh. A well-fed child is a healthy child. I will talk to you later."

"Okay, ma, bye. Love you."

"Love you, too," she replied, ending the call with a

deep exhale.

***

The next day at work wasn't any different for Mo; she arrived on time to work, did the usual ward rounds, and attended to patients. She had stopped at Teju's bed earlier during the day, and from his chart, she could tell he had awakened during the night, although he had been put back to sleep judging from the scribbled writing of Doctor Okeke.

The day dragged on, as it always did. By noon, Mo's legs were aching from the constant movement. She had just gotten a chance to rest her feet and was daydreaming about when it would finally be her turn on the rooster to be in the Emergency room.

At least I wouldn't have to be on my feet as often there since I just need to attend to emergency cases, which mostly revolved around treating cuts, patients with sudden illness and not so often, stabilizing patients that have been in an accident, she thought as Dunni arrived from the wards.

"Mo, your attention is required at Ward 8," she said, taking a seat next to her and dragging out her lunch bag from under the table.

"Oh, what happened again?" Mo asked, her lips set in a thin line, and a frown was beginning to form on her face. "I just finally got to sit down since nah."

Dunni laughed empathetically, "Pele, but I think it's

that emergency case yesterday. The man's family is here. Doctor Olufade already attended to them, but he said I should call you since you attended to him yesterday. You know Doctor Atinuke doesn't come on Wednesdays, and Nurse Tomiwa from ER is on leave today."

"Oh okay, no wahala then. Thank you." Mo said, her frown turning to a tight smile. Family members always wanted updates, reassurance, and sometimes even hope, and while she wasn't always sure of what to say to them, her empathy and years of experience always kicked in whenever she was in such a situation. But with Tejumola's family, she wasn't sure she would know what to say to them; she couldn't place why, but she just felt like it would be different.

Mo made her way to the ward, mentally preparing herself for the encounter. When she arrived, a woman who seemed to be in her late fifties sat on a plastic chair beside the bed, her eyes red from crying, and a younger man who looked to be in his thirties, with a striking resemblance to Tejumola stood beside her, his fingers clamped around her right shoulder in reassurance. Doctor Olufade stood at the other side of the bed.

"…will be fine. He was sedated because he was a bit disoriented when he woke up earlier, and he needs the rest to help him recover," he was saying as he noticed her.

"This is Nurse Mo. She was part of the nurses that

assisted in the surgery yesterday. If you need anything, you can always reach out to her, but you can be assured that he will be fine."

"All right. Thank you, doctor," the man beside the woman said.

Doctor Olufade nodded his head and excused himself.

Mo plastered a small smile on her face as he walked away and turned to Tejumola's family. "Good afternoon, I am Nurse Mo," she said politely.

The man nodded. "Nice to meet you, ma'am. I am his brother, and this is our mother."

"Good afternoon ma," she repeated again, directly to the woman this time.

The woman nodded and managed to give Mo a small smile.

"The doctor has already assured us that he'd be fine, but we would like to know more about what happened and also what we can get or what he needs to make him more comfortable."

Mo nodded, and with carefully chosen words, she informed his family about all they wanted to know.

After Mo informed Tejumola's family of what they needed to know, his brother left immediately to get some of the items she had mentioned after requesting that his brother be transferred to a private ward while his mother stayed with him. Mo returned to her station, and the rest of the evening was a blur.

***

Tejumola

Mo was scanning Tejumola's chart during her ward round the next morning when Tejumola opened his eyes. He squinted his eyes as he tried to adjust to the bright light in the room. He had the faint recollection of waking up earlier during the night, and he had been able to speak to his mother briefly before the drugs knocked him out again.

His entire body hurt, and it felt like he had been in every sense of the phrase, "wrecked over by a train.".. He noticed a nurse at the foot of his bed; as he tried to get a better sense of the room, she hadn't noticed he was awake, and her face was stern.

He didn't know why, but he had a huge urge to make her smile. He tried to speak, but his throat was extremely dry, and all he could manage was a faint, raspy sound. Mo turned then, rushing to his side. She assesses his condition and tries hard not to stare into his eyes, which are now on her face, as she checks his vitals. Once she was certain he was stable, she raised up his bed with the lever and helped him drink some water.

"Hi, I am Nurse Mo," she said. "How do you feel?"

"Good."

"Are you sure you don't feel pain anywhere?"

"I do. I feel about as much pain as someone who has just had an accident."

"Oh…" Mo said, trying hard to stop the smile that

was beginning to form on her face.

"Okay, but can you rate it on a scale of 1 to 10." She said, with an empathetic smile, and the only thing that ran through his mind was how pretty she looked with her smile.

"Six," he responded, trying not to wince as he mentally blocked out the pain. Every part of his body hurt, but it was better than the first time he woke up; he hadn't even been able to move without feeling as if every part of him was on fire.

"Okay, I would administer some pain relief for you," she said.

"Please, nothing that would make me sleep again, ooh. I am tired of sleeping," he said playfully.

"Okay, sir."

"Thank you, ma."

She offered a small smile. She had moved to his other side, and her entire attention was on his IV fluids.

"Where's my mum?"

"She stepped out to get something to eat. She should be back soon. Your brother was also here yesterday," she responded. There was something soothing about her words; perhaps it was years of practice in caring for patients or the way she had added that his brother had also been here to check up on him, even though he hadn't asked. It felt like she was telling him that he wasn't alone.

"All right," he exhaled.

She nodded, "I would be back to administer some pain relief. In the meantime, I hope you don't need anything."

"Actually, I do."

"Oh, okay. What do you need?"

"Could you keep me company till my mum gets back?"

He watched her reaction as he spoke. It went from shock, fluster, and confused to uncertainty. He had always been a good judge of character, and from the moment he opened his eyes till this moment, he could tell she was the kind of person he wanted to get to know. He knew when she made her decision from the way she suddenly pursed her lips and took a silent inward breath.

"I can't stay with you for too long because I have other patients to attend to, but I can stay a while till I am sure you can be left alone."

He smiled, relieved. "Thank you."

"But I have to go and get you that pain relief first; I will be back soon," she said abruptly as she walked to the door.

"But I can do without..." he started, but she was already out of the door.

***

Mo

Mo was back in a few minutes. She smiled at him as she

came in, and Tejumola watched as she expertly clamped the IV tube, and with methodical and precise motions, she wiped the injection port with a cotton swab and inserted the pre-filled syringe into the injection port with steady hands. She proceeded to carefully withdraw the needle, covering it with the safety cap, before disposing it in the bin beside the bed. Then, she released the clamp to allow the IV fluids to resume their journey.

Tejumola studied her as she moved from the drip stand to sit beside him on a plastic chair.

"So, is there anything I can do for you, sir?"

"No, I am good. Thank you," he mumbled, smiling. "Pardon my manners. I am Teju."

"Nice to meet you, Tejumola," Mo said with a wide smile.

His attentive eyes caught her smile, "What is funny?"

"Nothing, you have a nice name. That's all."

"So, Mo…" he started and then hesitated.

"Yes?"

"What does it mean? Is it a nickname?" he asked, holding back a yawn and trying to ignore his fast-beating heart. The injection was kicking in, and he was feeling sleepy again. He wondered if the injection was aiding his body to take back the rest he had missed out on from the countless sleepless nights he had in the past few months or if the drugs just kicked in that fast.

"Yeah, it is sort of a nickname, but it is also a short version of my name."

"Oh, what is it? Moyinoluwa?" he guessed, yawning.

Mo smiled, "Not even close. And you should get some rest."

"Did you do this on purpose. I thought I told you I don't want something that would make me sleep."

"I didn't do anything. I think you are just too tired," Mo insisted.

He smiled sleepily and tried again. "All right. Is it Mofiyinfoluwa?"

She shook her head. "No."

"Moyosore?" he tried again, struggling to keep his eye open

"No, Tejumola. It is Mofeyisopefoluwa. Now rest."

"Nice name," he murmured as she got up. She walked out as he drifted to sleep.

★★★

Tejumola found Mo interesting. She looked young, but she also carried out her job with such efficiency that one would think she had over two decades of experience doing it. He wanted to speak to her again and stare into her striking brown eyes, which seemed to communicate more than her mouth did. He hadn't had a chance to talk to her alone ever since he woke up a week ago; it was either he was with his mom, a friend, or his brother.

The one time he managed to be alone, another nurse attended to him. He hoped she would be the one to check on him this evening, he could manage to move around by himself now without too much pain, so he had told his mum to go home for the night. All living deities must have heard his prayers because Mo walked in just in time.

He smiled.

"Well, hello, Nurse Mo. I was starting to think you have abandoned me."

Mo laughed. "Abandon? No way, I can never abandon my patient."

"Okay, oh."

"I see you are alone today. Where is your mum?" Mo asked.

He grinned. *She noticed.* He had assumed that he was the only one who wished they could be alone every time she walked through the door.

"I told her to go home. I am a full-grown man so she doesn't need to be here every second of the day. Besides, she needs to rest, " he replied.

Mo glanced at the chart at the foot of his bed. "Oh, okay. And how do you feel today?"

"I am good, Mo." He replied, smiling.

Mo nodded and smiled, saying, "That's good. I just wanted to check on you. I will leave you to it then."

He stared at her with hopeful eyes. "Can you stay

with me for a while?"

Mo's eyes narrowed. "Hmmm, why?"

"You want the truth?"

Mo nodded her head in response.

"Because I want to get to know you. I don't know why or what it is about you, but from the moment I woke up and saw you, I just felt like we'd hit it off well."

"Ooo...kkk...ay," Mo said, squinting.

"And if I might add, you have the prettiest pool of brown eyes I have ever seen," Teju admitted.

Mo smiled and slanted her head. "Thank you."

"You are welcome. So, what do you say? Can you sit with me for a while?"

"I should be on my way home, but I can stay a while," Mo murmured, grinning.

"So, there is something I have always been curious about." Teju began, tapping the space beside him on the single couch in the room for her to sit.

"What is that?" Mo asked, taking a seat beside him.

"My mum mentioned that you were part of the team that did my surgery. I thought only doctors did surgery."

Mo laughed. "Really?"

"Don't judge me. I know nothing about the medical setting. I deal with designs and construction, nothing remotely close to saving human lives," Teju said, slightly embarrassed.

With a smile still on her face, Mo said, "Well, you are not totally wrong, don't worry. Not all nurses are qualified to help in surgery, but I am a registered nurse with experience in surgical nursing. So, I sometimes assist as a scrub nurse in the operating room."

"Oh wow, that's impressive," Teju replied, astonished.

A modest smile graced Mo's face, "Not as impressive as you, Mr Principal Architect."

"Oh, you saw that. It's really just a title. The job hasn't changed much from what it was when I was a designer. It is just more workload and ensuring everyone is doing the right thing."

He thought of the workload that would have piled up on his desk now that he was hospitalized.

"Okay, but at least you enjoy what you do, right?" Mo asked.

"I do, but we all know this country makes everything harder than it should be," he says, launching into his current dilemma at work. He tells Mo about the government infrastructure his company is bidding for but is close to losing because a competitor has resorted to bribery despite their design plans not being as concrete as theirs.

Mo sighed in resignation when he finished narrating his plight: "This country and corruption, I am so tired."

He laughed humorlessly, "They are inseparable, and if one keeps talking about Nigerian issues, one would never stop." He paused thoughtfully. "What do you like to do for fun?"

Mo thought about it, she hadn't done anything fun in a long time. She spent most of her time at work, and her Sundays and leave over the past one year had been spent catching up on sleep, watching movies, and poring over work applications and emails. "I am not sure."

He simply nodded. "I enjoyed talking with you, and I don't know if you'd be willing to go see a movie with me after I am discharged, and after that, dinner, and hopefully, after that, several other dates."

Mo blushed, "Hmmm... but you know you aren't in the physical condition to be going up and down, even after being discharged, right?"

"Well, that is why I have my own personal Nurse Mofeyisopefoluwa."

Mo laughed, "You would pay for the service, ooh."

"I don't mind, as long as it means I have you beside me," he said, with a huge grin on his face.

Mo laughed harder. "I hear you, ooh. Shaa keep in mind that I am expensive."

He nodded. "So, what do you say, Mo?"

"Yes."

"Yes?" he asked, unsure.

Mo nodded again.

"So, does that mean I can have your number?" he asked, already picking up his phone.

"Sure."

"Thank you," he said, grateful and relieved.

Mo
★★★

Mo smiled as she went through her messages later that night. She had an extra message from someone else for a change. She pondered on their conversation from when she walked into his room. He sounded polite enough, but as a young nurse, she always tried not to cross the boundaries with her male patients. Yet, in recent times, she has found that she was always willing to jump over the damn boundaries for Tejumola.

She had expected him to comment on how boring her life must be or how odd it was she didn't know what she loved to do, but there was nothing of such. Instead, he said:

"I enjoyed talking with you, and I don't know if you'd be willing to go see a movie with me after I am discharged, and after that, dinner, and hopefully, after that, several other dates."

During the next few days before his discharge, she and Tejumola texted every night, and her encounters with him during her shift became the highlight of her day. They grew closer as Teju progressively recovered. At night, they would share personal stories over texts, and sometimes, he would choose calling over texting.

It was one of those nights when Mo told him about her plans to relocate.

"What is that one thing you are very passionate about, aside from your job?".

She hesitated, her gaze drifting to her muted TV. "Well, I'm passionate about making a difference in people's lives. It's why I became a nurse. But beyond that, I've always wanted to travel and experience what it feels like to meet people from different walks of life."

"Hmmm..." Teju said she could almost imagine him nodding his head thoughtfully. "That sounds wonderful. So, have you ever been anywhere else aside from Nigeria?"

"Hmm, I visited Jamaica and South Africa for work one time. I don't know if that counts."

"It does," Teju answered.

"What about you? Have you been anywhere except Nigeria?" she curiously asked.

"Yes, I actually love to travel. It is one of the things I do when I am on break or on leave." .

"Really?"

"Yes, I have been to about six states in the US, Greece, Kenya, Spain, and Peru, and I did my master's program in the UK."

"Wow, really?" she gasped, shocked.

Teju chuckled. "Maybe it is because we both love to travel that you feel so familiar."

"I do?" Mo's heart skipped a beat, surprised at how

she felt the same way about him.

"Yes, it is strange, but I feel like I have known you for longer than just a few days."

"I guess it is just one of those things. Sometimes, we meet people and instantly feel like we have known them forever."

"I guess life has a funny way of bringing people together," Teju agreed. "Talking about travelling, where's the first place you envision you visiting outside Nigeria?" He asked.

She paused, "The US," she said after a while. "I have actually been working on relocating for a long time, and it seems like it would be happening any moment from now."

"Wow, that's incredible," Teju said with genuine admiration.

"Thank you," she said a bright smile on her face.

"So, you are part of the Japa culture, too. I am starting to think I am literally the only youth left in this Nigeria that isn't planning to relocate."

She laughed, "I am sure you are not."

"Yeah? I think not because literally all my friends have relocated."

"I don't know, and I can't speak for others, but Nigeria is not an enabling environment. It kills dreams, and aside from that, I think I have had my fair share of corruption and bribery, bad roads, lack of infrastructure, and don't even get me started on terrible work ethics and the meagre salaries."

Teju sighed. "I get. That honestly is an issue. Whenever I travel, I always experience some sort of culture shock because everything is just so different. Customer service, infrastructure, to availability of immediate needs, there is a plan for everything."

"Exactly. I just want a simple life, where I can afford to pay my bills and live my life without worrying about basic things like electricity, bad roads, or if the price of fuel is going to go up the next day without any legit reason," she confessed.

"Honestly, our government need to do better. Lack of basic needs is what is making a lot of people relocate," Teju added.

She shook her head even though he couldn't see her, "It is not only the government. The people also play a part. Because there is no rule or law governing everyone, everyone is now also doing as they see fit. For instance, the other day, I was at the bank to cash a cheque, and the accountant at the counter told me for him to attend to me on that day, I had to give him 'something.'" She said rapidly.

Teju laughed. "For real?"

"Yes, he insisted that I had to give him money before I could cash the cheque, and I was just confused because wasn't that what he was being paid to do."

Teju sighed. "We honestly need to do better as Nigerians."

They continued talking, sharing stories and dreams, and the hours seemed to pass in the blink of an eye. Teju soon realised that he found solace in her company, and Mo felt an unexpected comfort in his presence. It was as if, despite the chaos of her daily life, she had found a moment of peace.

***

Mo had just gotten home and switched on her mobile data when she saw the mail that she had always dreamed about getting.

"Congratulations…" it reads.

Mo's heart raced as she read the mail; it had been five weeks since she did the interview, and with each passing day, her anxiety skyrocketed that perhaps she had done something wrong. Unsure of what to do first, Mo dialed her mother's number to tell her the good news.

"Congratulations, my dear. Finally, I am so happy, " her mum said, as she broke into tears of joy.

After speaking with her dad and texting her brother, she tried but failed to slow her racing heart before dialing Teju's number. It had been almost three months since the accident that brought him into her life.

"Hi, beautiful," he said, picking on the first ring.

Mo smiled shyly. "Hello."

"Did you just get in? How are you?" Teju asked.

"I am fine. Guess what?" she asked.

"Hmmm, what?" He asked.

"You are supposed to guess it."

"Oh, okay. Hmmm, you got the job," he guessed.

"Oh my God! You got it right," she yells into the speaker.

"God, he loves it when she is happy. I told you it was coming, didn't I? You were just getting worked up for no reason."

She smiled. Ever since she had the interview, she had become panicky and suspected she had made a mistake and lost her shot at getting the job. Once, during their conversation, she had randomly said:

'I think I made a mistake when she asked me how I would ensure clear communication with a patient and the patient's family.'

And rather than get angry that she wasn't paying attention to whatever he had been saying beforehand, he had simply said, 'That's you overthinking it, Mo. You are a wonderful nurse, and I am sure you did well. You would get the job.' before easing her back into the discussion.

"Yes, you did," Mo agreed with a nod.

"So, what do you say about a congratulatory dinner? Can my nurse give me the pass to do that much now?"

"Hmmm... let's see." She pretended to think about it. "Definitely cleared to take me out to dinner."

"Great. It's a date then."

"Yeah, but can we make it after I get my visa?" she

asked suddenly.

"Most definitely."

★★★
Teju & Mo

Meeting up with Teju outside the hospital was so different from what Mo had ever imagined; she had never imagined that a day would come in her life when she would feel so happy to be around someone. She arrived at the restaurant he had chosen because she had insisted that he probably knew better spots than she did since she spent most of her days indoors.

Yet, it seemed exactly like somewhere she would have chosen. The restaurant's understated elegance shone through soft lighting, minimalist décor, and polished wooden tables, creating the perfect inviting and refined ambiance. She spotted Teju as she stepped in. It was easy enough with the confident and vibrant aura he exuded. His captivating brown eyes drew her in just like the first time she had seen his ID card as he smiled at her across the room. She walked to the table, and he was already on his feet to help pull out her chair.

"Oh my God, you look stunning," he said, appreciating the yellow evening gown she wore, paired with a white stiletto.

"Thank you." Mo smiled shyly. "You look good too."

"Thank you, Nurse Mo," Teju said playfully as he

dragged out her chair. Once she was seated, Teju moved to his seat opposite her. Getting to know her over the past months had made him realise that she was who he wanted, but he hadn't told her. *Not yet*, he'd thought. Hoping to let her settle into the idea of him before he brought up anything serious. *For now, he was quite content being her special friend*, he'd thought a week later, but not anymore.

"So, I waited for you so you could order because I didn't know what you'd like."

"Oh, thank you," she said, touching her heart. "Hmmm, let me just scan through their menu."

After a few minutes of deliberation, she decided on the *Penne Arrabbiata* pasta, she thought it looked nice. She scanned the menu for a minute again and agreed on vegetable salad to accompany her meal and citrus punch, for her choice of drink.

"Okay, I am ready to order," she announced, looking up to catch Teju's eyes staring intensely at her.

She looked away, stunned at the intensity in his eyes.

Teju smiled. "God, you are so beautiful."

"Thank you," she replied, trying hard to control the huge smile on her face.

"You are welcome. God dey create shaa," Teju said as he beckoned the waiter.

She laughed as the waiter approached them. After placing her order, Teju ordered the same thing but opted for a spritz instead of a citrus punch.

"So, how is the preparation to relocate?" Teju asked as soon as the waiter walked away.

"Good. I told you I have to resume in three months, right?"

He smiled. Her tone had gone up a notch from excitement. "Yes, you did."

"Yeah, so I am stopping work at the end of the month to have enough time to prepare."

"Okay, have you gotten your tickets?" Teju asked, his heart beating fast. He only hoped she wouldn't be angry, rushed, or pressured with what he had done.

"Not yet, but I plan to buy it very soon because the earlier the better," she said, thinking about the cost of the ticket.

"Hmmm... what if I told you you don't need to purchase a flight ticket because I already got us tickets," Teju said nervously.

"Awwn, you did." Mo smiled brightly. "Wait, what? Us?" she asks as confusion flittered across her face.

"Yes, us, Mo," Teju started. "I am well aware that it has just been three months since we met, but I knew deep down since the first time I woke up to you at the foot of my bed that I want to be with you. I like you, no scratch. I am sure I am in love with you, Mo. I am not asking you to dedicate to anything serious right now until you are well settled, but I wanted to let you know that I am willing to travel with you and help you settle for the first few months if you would let me."

Mo watched him as he spoke, and a huge smile broke across her face when he was done. This was everything she had always wanted, to find someone who was her type of person and to be in an enabling environment that would help her grow. She reached out for his hands across the table.

"I like you too, Teju, and I want you to travel with me. Let's travel together," Mo said.

Teju smiled in relief, and to Mo, his eyes shined even brighter than ever. "Thank you, Mo. I promise not to let you down," he promised, sealing the promise with a kiss on her hand.

"You had better not," Mo said jokingly. "Now tell me, since when have you been planning this?"

Teju laughed softly at her curiosity. "Since you first told me about moving to the US. I applied for a visiting visa, and because I have been there a number of times, it was approved. I think they trust me enough to come back after a while."

Mo giggled. "But what about work?"

"Well, I am due for leave. So, I thought that I must have been saving it for this without knowing and I can pretty much work remotely for now. I trust my team enough to do that."

Mo gave him a knowing look, "You have this all figured out, don't you?"

"No, you made me figure it out," he said with a soft

smile as the waiter arrived with their meal.

"Ma'am, Sir, we are sorry it took a while," the waiter said, but they both simply waved his apology away with a smile.

Mo watched Teju as he dug into his meal and realised that she might have assumed that Nigeria wasn't an enabling environment for her, but it was what had enabled her to meet him. She knew as she began to eat that she might not be able to predict the future, but she liked him as much as he liked her, and that was enough for her. He was a keeper, and she made herself a promise to do everything within her power to keep him, no matter what it takes.

Zainab O. Bankole was born in the vibrant and ever-bustling city of Lagos, Nigeria, where she grew up in a lively household with her three sisters. As the second of four girls, she developed a strong sense of family and resilience, both of which fuel her creativity and leadership skills. A self-proclaimed hopeless romantic, Zainab's passion for love stories shines through in both her writing and reading choices. She enjoys exploring the complexities of human relationships, infusing her narratives with emotion and authenticity.

When Zainab isn't immersed in the world of books or crafting her own stories, you can find her indulging in Nollywood movies, where her love for vibrant storytelling continues. With a natural gift for leadership, Zainab has been known to take charge, whether it's organizing community events or championing women's empowerment. Her infectious optimism, coupled with her dedication to her craft, has made her a rising star in the world of African fiction and a voice to watch for in the literary scene.

Ogu

Mary-Ella E

The hassles and bustles of the people of Rumuoyi village were at its peak in preparation for Ogu - the festival of a year's transition; its people were everywhere taking old stuff out of their huts or taking new things in - as was the tradition. It was the busiest day in Rumuoyi village. At midnight of the last day of the year, old things are taken to Esezi in the heart of the village, and everyone would, at the cusp of dawn, surround their old things in a large bonfire and chant the old saying:

'Year young, year old,
last day, last day
go with your troubles,
go with the past,
go with our pains.
stay with our past.

The drummers worked the song into a frenzy as they danced around the fire as it engulfed the things of the past year. It was believed to take the past pains with the dying fire. This began the Ogu festival. The following day, the dawn of the new year, they'd all return for the dance with the Ogu drum.

Nkasi-obi, a woman past her prime, dusted a beautiful velvet trouser suit that was laid out on her mattress with a dusting rag and smiled. She had practically cried her husband-to-be into paying for the all-too-expensive suit her husband-to-be had complained but still, come succumbed to her demands. He wasn't rich or anything, so the suit wasn't what he had wanted to use the salary he had worked so hard for.

Admiring her suit, she smiled once more. It was almost time; she looked at her husband-to-be's watch on the desk beside her.

Wait till they see me. They'll know my future husband is from the city, especially that stupid Mbechi. Mbechi had been a rival from childhood. Anything Nkasi-obi got, Mbechi got a better version of it, but not this, not him, not her Chibuike.

She smiled contently.

"Eleven forty-two," she thought aloud.

By then, the villagers were all at Esezi; some sitting, some standing, chitter-chatter from every open corner - everyone was happy. Nkasi-obi had finished getting dressed, her husband-to-be was relieved and gave her several compliments.

"Although you stress me out sometimes, my love for you will never be stressed," Chibuike finally said - It was practically his mantra for her.

Nkasi-obi smiled at him.

They hugged and were startled by the eruption of voices and the heating of metal tins, raising a cacophony of various echoes around them. They smiled knowingly at each other and joined the cheer.

"Happy new year," they chorused as neighbours greeted neighbours, people hailed each other, admiring and dissenting their outfits, weather and hopes.

The Otu-Elulu eulogised the families, from their ancestors to the newest born. That family danced around him until he finished and moved to the next family to do the same, and they'd react the same way. When everyone had processed to Esezi, the drummers went to their designated spot at the Ogu drum.

The Ogu drums were stacked in a rack of steps with the biggest at the bottom; what held them together was a mystery to all except the drummers; even the selection of the drummers was a mystery. It was a thing of envy to play the drums and beyond beauty to listen to. These drums were raised in secret and on only three occasions: the death of the Nyeweli, Ogu Festival, in times of war. The drums were the major tourist attraction for Rumuoyi.

Nkasi-obi watched the dancers from neighbouring villages sweat and laugh, the fire dancers play with fire as if it was nothing, the masquerades chased children and young women, the array of assorted food on the tables spread wide enough to feed a nation, the elders whispering amongst themselves, then the Nyeweli dance into Esezi all his glory with his wives forming an emblem around him, soon after that Onye-Ozi'agbara with his minions hovering around and over him as he marched to the heart of Esezi.

Nkasi-obi's joy wasn't from the excitement that came with greeting the new year. It wasn't from the celebration or the splendid view. It was the fact that she had just gotten engaged, and the thought of it alone summoned butterflies in her stomach.

After so many years.

Nkasi-obi chuckled and sighed.

Finally, a bride I will be.

Nkasi-obi eyed her soon-to-be husband and smiled just as her stomach complained loudly.

Chibuike tried to disguise a laugh as he wrinkled his face, staring at her stomach.

"Let me just visit the food table for a second," Nkasi-obi mumbled. "Need anything?"

Chibuike shook his head in reply.

Nkasi-obi went towards the serving women but stopped dead in her tracks when she saw Mbechi and then made a full 360 degrees turn.

"Not now abeg," Nkasi-obi whispered to herself. Remembering the suit, she had put on for display, she turned right back and continued her strut towards the massive table.

Mbechi, who was at the large table and pouring herself a drink, tilted her head, and with a small smile, drawled, "Oh, is that Nkasi I see? Nkasi-obi?"

"It's me o!" Nkasi-obi retorted dryly as she picked a flat earthenware bowl and handed it to one of the serving women.

"I would say you don't look a day over fifty, but I'd be lying," Mbechi muttered and tried to get something out of her teeth.

Upset, Nkasi-obi pursed her lips. She exhaled and concentrated on the woman who was serving her but couldn't hold her tongue. "At least, I'm still beautiful enough to earn this outfit from my husband."

Mbechi smirked. "No outfit is enough to hide those wrinkles. And please, don't be silly. He's not your husband yet. You people haven't even done your traditional wedding." She laughed loudly, drawing the attention of the people nearby. "He's just looking for one of these young maidens to marry o! With you, he's just buying himself time, and time is what you don't have, my dear."

Nkasi-obi fumed and spat, "How dare you talk to me in that manner?"

"My dear, you're still a 'miss', and I am a 'Mrs', expecting another one soon too." Mbechi sneered, rubbing her swollen belly. "So, we are not mates."

Nkasi-obi watched Mbechi take out a serviette to wipe her hands and mouth and wrinkled her nose when Mbechi burped.

Mbechi made to leave, dropped her serviette in Nkasi-obi's food then covered her mouth in fake surprise. "Oops! Being pregnant sure makes you clumsy."

"Mbechi," Nkaso-obi cried.

Mbechi flicked her hair at her and hummed as she waltzed away.

Nkasi-obi pulled her back by the hair. "Don't ever in your life speak to me like that or I will injure you."

Mbechi stared blankly at Nkaso-obi, then picked a knife from the table and thrust it at Nkasi-obi. Nkasi-obi had expected Mbechi's action, but it had happened so fast that there were two slits on the side of her suit.

Beyond anger and pain, Nkasi-obi pounced on Mbechi and beat her all the way to the centre of the celebration. The drummers stopped abruptly, making their fight more obvious to the large crowd. A mixture of shock, amusement and disgust were on the faces in the crowd as Nkasi-obi made an attempt to fill a pregnant woman's mouth with sand. The Nyeweli's guards intervened and took them away.

Nkasi-obi was put in a separate room because Mbechi was *afraid* of staying in the same room with a *madwoman* who beats up 'pregnant women'. She could see the door to the chamber room of the elders, and she could also see her husband-to-be, alongside a woman she could recognise from a mile away, her soon-to-be mother-in-law. They were judging her case. She had broken two rules:

'You can't lay your hands on a pregnant woman.' – it's a taboo.

'You can never and should never fight in Esezi, especially on market days and special occasions such as Ogu' – it's forbidden.

Nkasi-obi prayed silently that the judgement wouldn't be harsh or expensive. A while later, a guard came to get her. The elders had given their verdict: a chicken, a goat, a few hot drinks and a fine for the treatment of the pregnant woman. She tried not to roll her eyes as no fine was given to Mbechi.

Annoyed, Nkasi-obi's father cut down the requirement of the bride price so she could leave the village at once. When they got to the car, her mother-in-law started lamenting.

"Look at the shame!!!" Nkasi-obi's mother-in-law

started. "The disgrace! Never ever have we had a case like this to settle. Not in this family. Not in *my* family," her mother-in-law spat, then turned menacing eyes to Nkasi-obi, who lowered her gaze.

She stared at the two slashes on the suit and the dirt; the suit was barely recognisable. She had wanted it so badly, to impress everyone so badly. It had cost a fortune.

Oh! I showed off alright!

Chibuike drove, his mother beside him, Nkasi-obi in the back like a reject.

"God is showing this boy a sign, and he is turning a blind eye," Nkasi-obi's mother-in-law sighed woefully. "God is telling you not to go through with this! What are the odds that on Ogu, something like this, which has never happened, if I may add, has happened?"

Nkasi-obi's mother-in-law sighed, moaned, and continued in her woeful opinions and pining, while Nkasi-obi looked outside, and Chibuike drove the car carefully, face emotionless, staring straight ahead, without a word uttered except when stole glances at Nkasi-obi and winked or smiled at her. As soon as the car came to a halt at Chibuike's house in the city, Nkasi-obi's mother-in-law went into the house with arms flailing and blaming her late husband for leaving her to do a man's job.

Nkasi-obi, still ashamed, climbed out of the car with her head down and walked into the house and sat in the darker part of the parlour. She was expecting 'anything' at this point; his yelling would be the highest point of her stress, but she would take it. It was her fault for walking into Mbechi's trap.

Chibuike watched Nkasi-obi go into the house and exhaled heavily. He climbed out of his car, brought out Nkasi-obi's suitcases and locked the car. He went straight to his bedroom and didn't find her. He finally found her in the parlour. His mother was beside her, chewing cashew nuts and began to moan her existence when she saw him. He ignored his mother and went to Nkasi-obi, slipped his hands in hers and pulled her up, then guided her to their room, where he wiped her eyes of any evidence of tears.

"I'm always the last. In school, I was the last to get picked, in my grades, in buying anything, for school fees even," she sobbed.

Chibuike held her when she burst into tears.

"In the university, I just barely got out, and Mbechi was always there to remind me of what I didn't have," Nkasi-obi paused, then continued, "Things changed when I moved out of this village. I got a good job, but then I was old, or old-er. The villagers made it their duty to remind me every day. No one took that duty more seriously than Mbechi."

Chibuike rubbed her back, urging her to go on.

"Seeing her today reminded me of all those memories, of every time my mother would call me a bad omen, and I lost it. I let it get the best of me. I disappointed everyone, disappointed myself, proving the things that my mother said," Nkasi-obi sniffed and wiped her eyes. "Maybe your mother was right."

Chibuike cupped her face and raised it, so he could look into her eyes.

"I don't know who said all those things to you, but I guess they're the ones with the bad luck. Ever since I met you, you've been the only good thing. My good luck charm and my happiness. Only your stress that used to tire me." Chibuike grinned, smoothing the cheeks with the back of his hands. "Although you stress me out sometimes, my love for you will never be stressed."

Nkasi-obi smiled. A smile of relief, of love. She now believed his love was true.

"That girl will see you next time and head for the hills. You fight like a mad person."

They laughed.

"You really like mad people o," Nkasi-obi mocked.

"So, you even know sey you mad sef," Chibuike jested.

"I can't wait for the next Ogu festival," Nkasi-obi said.

"Ha! We just entered a new year, my dear, relax! But hopefully, next year, you'll be the next pregnant woman, not the one that beat them up," Chibuike said, smiling.

"Will you ever let me live this down?" Nkasi-obi asked, wrinkling her face.

"Never o! We'll even name our first child Ogu," Chibuike blurted out, laughing, Nkasi-obi she joined him while attempting to use the pillow to swat him, and he covered his face in defence.

Mary-Ella E. is a Biochemistry undergraduate and hopes to remind women of the strength they have within them through writing. She loves reading and spends most of her free time as a photographer and makeup artist.

Mary-Ella E. is a science graduate with a passion for the creative arts, blending her love for photography and the refinement of makeup artistry. Though her background is rooted in science, she has discovered writing as a subtle yet fulfilling addition to her creative pursuits. Raised by a single mother, Mary-Ella believes that resilience is a fundamental human requirement, a belief that strongly influences her approach to both life and art.

Her photography captures the world in its most beautiful and raw forms, while her makeup artistry showcases the power of transformation and self-expression. These creative outlets allow her to explore the intersection of science and art, where structure meets beauty. Writing, for her, has become a natural extension of this creative journey, offering her another way to tell stories and express herself.

Whether behind the camera, working with a makeup brush, or crafting words on a page, Mary-Ella's work is driven by her belief in the power of resilience and creativity. She finds joy in constantly evolving her passions and sharing them with the world, embracing every opportunity to grow and refine her craft.

Marriage on the Brink

Olayemi Oyin

I once assumed that 'for better for worse' was just a cliché people say at the altar. But as I sit in the fully air-conditioned room of Eko Hotel and Suites, I know it's a warning, telling you to tread softly because there'd be slippery grounds in every marriage that could make you cry your eyes out.

The pristine walls and interior design are a testament to the copious financial resources, work, and time bequeathed to it. The biting taste of bitterness curled up my throat like a slow-rising mist, leaving a metallic tang on my tongue. I shrugged, failing to resist the tears that were building in my eyes. How I wished my life was as smooth as the allure of the room. I was serenaded with bittersweet memories.

I caressed the portable sonic radio – Timi's gift. It sat mute on the dressing table. I pressed the 'on' button, and it cackled to life.

"Happy Independence Day, my people," the presenter's soothing voice filled the room, but my heart threatened to split in misery like a feeble splinter of wood.

Then, King Sunny Ade's song *Oro Tolonlo* started to play. It was a song about loyalty and betrayal. The lyrics seeped into my soul, echoing the betrayals and heartaches of my past and bleeding memories I thought I had healed from. I bowed my head and wept sore like an infant in pain.

It was in this same hotel on October 1st, 2018 - on the day Nigeria celebrated her 58th year of independence - that I met Timi Gbadebo. I was reminded of how much I had missed the overwhelming love, laughter, and connection Timi and I shared. I finally realised I was wrong. Yes, I had always known there would be days of sunny smiles and booming laughter and days of tears and pain. Yes, pain, but not a gut-wrenching, searing pain because, you see, I've always believed that love conquers all. Or perhaps I thought.

As I sit here, wandering back into the jungle of long ago, I can't help but reflect on Timi's loyalty to me. I wished I was as committed to him, like the average Nigerian during the football season or the Olympics, glued to TV screens and praying fervently that the Super Eagles make us proud.

I wish I had a pint of the commitment that made our ancestors fight with their last drop of blood to see us enjoy the freedom we enjoy today. However, I've realised I was just like my past lovers and wasn't any better than them.

Perhaps, I was still healing, because why would my thought keep straying to my past relationships? Maybe I needed to think, I deserved the pain the memories my past brought. I needed to stare at the stark contrast between my past fiancés and Timi, my husband. I had pushed Timi away even though he was nothing short of an angel.

Lanre, my first love…

"Do you solemnly take this woman to be your lawfully wedded wife?" the priest had asked, successfully masking his impatience – he still had about two more weddings to officiate.

I chuckled, elated that I was finally getting married. But with Lanre's look, my joy withered like a dry leaf.

He shook his head in slow motion and didn't even tear up. "I'm sorry I can't do this." He whispered.

The officiating priest frowned, not sure he heard him right. "Can you be more audible?"

"I can't marry her."

I heard a grumble from the congregation, and the room began to spin. It felt like the world was crashing on me or more like a bullet lodged in my heart, slowly squeezing the life out of me. I thought I'd run mad. I couldn't remember when my back kissed the ground, but when I regained consciousness, I got a text from him.

"You're nothing better than infertile soil. Why bother with you?"

I just knew there was no point begging him. His mind was made up. I felt drenched in cold and stuck. At twenty-nine years of age, where do I start from? I couldn't talk or move for two weeks. I was messed up and completely drained of hope. How would I face my friends, relatives, and colleagues at work?

Wait, what do they say about one good turn deserving another?

I was solidly with this guy when he lost his well-paying job due to a fatal accident. When everyone left, I was the only one standing, cleaning up faeces and urine for two good years before he finally recuperated. Why did he disappoint me? Well, why wouldn't he? It's like expecting a brim-filled basket of water because I've always known he wasn't the one from the first day he slapped me and looked me straight in the eyes and thundered:

"I will slap you again if you don't sit now!"

And I kept convincing myself he would come to realise my worth, I just had to stick around till he did. But he overlooked the gem that lay in me even before I shared with him the weight of my emotional baggage.

I felt pain pool in the pit of my stomach, my head throbbed. I was worthless.

A tear rolled down my face as I heaved a sigh. Well, what do they say about men named 'Lanre' being the devil's offspring? I had thought he wouldn't have the nerve to end things before mounting the altar. But I guess he took me by surprise and told me point-blank before the church congregation that he couldn't proceed with our union.

But even worse than Lanrre was Shola. Even though he never yelled at me, no matter what. He was literally a horny fowl. He couldn't look beyond every lady's boobs and bums. His gaze always hovered on my body, reducing me to a mere sensual object. Always commenting on the shape of my breasts and the curve of my hips.

"Babe, your breasts are as perky as a well-moulded Fufu."

"Babe, I can't wait to have a taste of you. You look tasty."

And then he would lick his lips to buttress his point while I fumed with silent anger.

But what hurt me the most was that he couldn't look beyond my past. The past of a rape victim who had to endure the trauma of abortion because she was too timid to report the unfortunate incident and ended up with an infected womb which was eventually removed. The pain felt fresh again. I wailed, clutching my chest in agony. He couldn't love me past my physical features. I was rather a burden even though I never chose to be a rape victim.

★★★

But Timi, my Timi, was as loyal as the shell of a snail, sticking with me against all odds. He has been my rock. Confidant. My everything.

I can still remember the formidable lines of anger drawn across Timi's forehead; his mouth coiled up in disappointment as he stormed out of my office five months ago. I haven't seen him since.

He was an 'ordinary' sales rep when I met him, earning peanuts as his monthly take home, but he was my heart's desire. Though, from a humble background, I believed he was the most thoughtful man on this planet. He had a beautiful heart so intentional about loving me.

Whenever I was worried, he'd share my concerns. If I was sick, he'd never leave my side, but nurse me until

I fully recovered. He constantly sent me surprise flowers and chocolates, anticipating my needs, and fulfilling them within the means of his modest income.

Timi accepted me even though I had emotional baggage and taught me to love myself again and hope for the best. He came into my life and plummeted my resolve to hold back on love. I don't think I could live without Timi. So, when he eventually popped the question:

"Will you marry me?"

I couldn't say no even though he had just one nice shirt and other fraying outfits. How could I? Not when he had become everything to me. I felt pain pool in the pit of my stomach, my head throbbed. I was worthless.

I sniffed, deliberately quenching the flood of self-pity that threatened to submerge me. Timi was a whole different game, not physically looking like my ideal man but had every virtue I ever looked out for in a man.

I knew he was the one on the first day I met him, which happened to be two months after Shola broke up with me. I couldn't get over him not with a piling breakup record and a brewing mental breakdown.

I cried everywhere. Anywhere. This time, I was walking down the hallway of this same Eko hotel and suites having gone there to rejuvenate. I felt someone tap me on my shoulder. I turned, obviously angry at the sudden intrusion into my moodiness which I'd worn like a cloak.

"I'm so sorry guess you're not used to being called Miss."

I lifted a brow and scrunched it into a frown. He had the sizable green, white, green flag with him. He was obviously celebrating independence. How I wished I had the strength to be so free and high spirited.

"What do you want Mister?" I asked, noticing the small Nigerian flag he held — a tribute to Independence Day.

Timi laughed, his right hand dipped into his rear pocket. "That sounded cocky. Happy Independence Day," he finally said.

When I didn't respond, he cleared his throat, in a futile bid to curb the air of awkwardness. I couldn't help but fix him a sorry smile which didn't reach my eyes.

He offered an understanding smile in return. "I'm sorry for the disturbance. But…I … I couldn't look past a crying lady."

I shrugged and posed a hostile demeanour. "What's so enthralling about a crying lady? Never seen one before?"

He stuttered, visibly confused but was quick to regain his composure. His words were soft yet sincere. "Are you fine? How can I help?"

Help? With what?

"Well, as you can see, I'm not. And if you truly want

to help you can give me a brand-new womb. Maybe Shola, my ex-boyfriend, would want to marry me then." I couldn't help the fresh burst of tears cascading down my face.

He reached for my hands uncertainly as my body shook with each wrecking tears, his features drawn in empathy. "I can't," he went on, lifted my chin so I was looking straight into his eyes. "But Jesus can."

I swear I could drown in the genuineness and innocence of the subtle uplift of his eyes. But I was angry. Angry he mentioned Jesus. Where was Jesus when those brutal animals had veered off the untarred and empty road of Ago Iwoye town not too far from the Olabisi Onabanjo University, packed the car, dragged me into the bush, and raped me one after the other?

Where was Jesus when Lanre disgraced me at the altar? Where was Jesus when Shola chose another lady over me because I have no womb? Maybe I was expecting too much from an unseen God.

"Where was he when the angels sent me to Nigeria?" I blurted instead.

Timi's face morphed into a puzzled one. "I don't understand."

My patience was waning. I shuffled my feet and raised my voice slightly, "If he couldn't keep away the rapists that destroyed my life, he could have at least prevented me from being born here in Nigeria. Maybe

I'd still have an intact womb."

"Oh, Nigeria." He nodded, realization setting in. "It can happen anywhere, you know. Nigeria is not to be blamed, and neither is Jesus," he added tentatively. "Some things are beyond human understanding, but we can always trust God to work things out for our good regardless of our experiences."

I swallowed my pain and distrust slowly. "I don't trust him."

"Okay."

Okay? I thought that was a weird response. Thankfully, he didn't sound like a preacher or prove to know everything. Infact, he was unassuming, but he embodied every good virtue. It endeared him to me, and I knew I just had fallen in love with him at that instant. But it was easy to blame it on my vulnerability.

He ensured he followed me to my door, consoled me without saying too much. His presence was enough for me and finally, he bade me goodnight after I felt much better.

He kept coming every single day but preferred to sit on the balcony where we could view passers-by and cars moving on as the day wearied.

Instead of running away, he stayed. From the little he said, he spoke more about God and unknown to me I started soaking them in and satisfying my curiosity about God, love and life by merely watching his lifestyle.

The day he popped the 'Will you marry me?' question, he got a better job.

"You see, you're my good luck charm," he said, pulling at my cheeks. "You're God's favour to me."

I believed him. Every word he spoke gave my life a new meaning and opened my eyes to my invaluable personality. I started to embrace myself again and see myself in a new light.

I embraced Jesus too and began to hope that maybe, just maybe I could still bear at least a child of my own. If Jesus could provide a well-paying job after agreeing in prayer with Timi over a couple of days, then he could intervene in my childbearing ability.

But the story didn't end there. It just started. My marriage was a dream come true for me because Timi was a perfect gentleman. So, I'd eventually find a man who could love me despite my scars.

Timi never made me feel inadequate but rather whole. He was head over heels for me just as I was for him.

His love for me was overwhelming, his patience, kindness and understanding made me feel secure, but I couldn't help but wonder how pale it still was compared to the greater love of God. Truly, all things work together for good to them who love God. I had everything at my beck and call: God, money, love and most especially the loyalty of my husband.

As days turned into weeks, and weeks into months.

I started to feel discontent. My light and joy started to grow dim, as I was still unable to conceive. Imagine having to endure the pitiable looks of friends and families. People always ready to give unsolicited advice as to why you're yet to conceive or having to attend the naming ceremony of your friend who got married after you and you're as barren as a bald head.

What about the negative pregnancy tests? a reminder of your dead womb and the never-ending cycle of hope and disappointment. Reality was beginning to set in. I would never understand the joy of safe delivery nor the pride of motherhood.

But I thought if I prayed and had faith well enough, everything would work out fine.

Everything seemed to be fine outwardly, but I couldn't help but notice the longing in Timi's eyes every time he greeted our neighbour's little son with his cute small eyes and cooing smiles. Or the day I told him I saw my period on the sixth month of our marriage, and he blurted.

"Again?" But quickly apologized and said it was a slip of tongue. I cried my eyes out that day.

Then I became desperate after the second year of marriage and societal pressure and family expectations mounted. The weight of my turmoil became too heavy to bear I started having terrifying nightmares.

I would wake up drenched in tears and sweat with visions of being childless forever. As the dreams intensified, so did my anxiety. I became so dependent on Timi and panicked every time he decided to go out. I feared he would leave me for another woman.

Unknown to me, I had developed separation anxiety disorder because I feared my husband was going to leave me one day to my fate.

If God couldn't stick around, what made me think my husband would? It was evident he loved children. We discussed children at the beginning of our marriage. We wanted two, we even had their names ready. But Timi didn't even want to discuss children anymore except I insisted, and I didn't even have the energy to try.

However, Timi still loved me, I would say even more deeply. He understood my anxiety and fear and would always console me. I often thought one day he would burst out in anger or exhaustion. But he never did.

Every single time he caught me moody or crying, he listened with rapt attention and prayed with me. Always quick to come back home so I don't feel too lonely. He'd bombard my phone with scriptures and encouraging messages. He didn't refrain from telling me every time about how much he loved me.

I'd ask, "Why?"

He'd simply reply, "Because I choose you."

Even when his mother suggested he married someone else in my presence, he stood his ground and rebuked his mother's misbehaviour respectfully, despite his mother's strictness. She had arrived one Sunday very angry and wouldn't even let me take her bag in and welcome her properly.

"Don't bother to cook anything, Sade. I won't eat," she said with a tone of finality, hissed and pushed me out of the way.

I was momentarily shocked. But I saw it as a responsibility to ensure she was okay. Maybe someone pissed her off on her way. So, I made my way to her room and knocked.

"Do you want to break the door? Barren woman! Leave my son alone and let him breathe!" She shrugged in irritation. "So, because of you I'd die without a grandson?"

I didn't know what to say, so I left her presence as quiet as a mouse. I cried my eyes out. It was like I was alone in the world and had no one to help me. How could Grandma be insensitive? Wasn't she a human too? The least she could have done was at least show some empathy. I was so troubled and restless. When my husband returned, she told him I was rude to her and called me all manner of names.

Despite all this, Timi was a solid support through it all. On a whim, he would just decide we go on vacation within Nigeria to unwind. He almost fought a woman in church, because she insinuated that I'd lived a promiscuous life in the past. I've never seen Timi that angry, but I did on that day. Even the pastor had to intervene knowing fully well that my husband was always easy going.

Then, one day I arrived at his office unaware, and I caught my husband with a fair lady seated gingerly on his lap, his arms wrapped around her waist and her lips on his. It was such an excruciating sight. I couldn't breathe. What I had constantly feared was finally happening before my very eyes. What do they say about premonitions becoming a reality? I didn't become angry, but I felt terribly sad, useless and defeated like a deflated tyre.

I turned and walked out of his office in slow motion. Timi muttered, "Babe, I can explain it's not what you think." But his voice sounded like a stranger's.

I moved out of our house that day. Surprisingly, after the initial surge of despair at Timi's office, I felt nothing but numbness.

The next day, he was at my office pleading, but I was unwilling to listen. However, he wouldn't leave unless I lent him attentive ears. I had no choice but to give in and invite him into my office to avoid creating a scene before my colleagues.

I had not even closed the door of my office behind me when he went down on his knees apologizing.

After successfully closing the door safely behind me, I walked towards my chair, sat and listened with rapt attention.

"I didn't kiss her, she forced herself on me. I have never cheated on you, and I never will."

After about a minute of deafening silence from me. I replied him and simply said, "I know you didn't."

"You know?" he whispered, surprised.

"I orchestrated everything. How could I watch you Timi suffer in silence and claim to truly love you? You deserve to carry and play with your own biological children. I can't deny you that."

An array of undecided emotions flickered across the ebbs of his eyes. Suddenly, he chuckled in dismay.

"Are you joking?"

"I'm sorry, Timi." I reached out to touch him, but his fiery glare made me shuffle my feet backward.

"Seriously? You'd do this to me, us, and God? Be...because of a child?" His jaw worked in anger, but he couldn't successfully rein it in. He kicked hard at my desk and barged out.

I knew better than to run after him. He had every right to be angry at me and his anger would even serve a good purpose. Our marriage was over. He deserved a woman who could give him children.

But who was I deceiving? The next month was hell. I heard nothing from Timi. He neither called nor texted me.

I thought of and dreamt about him every day. I began to regret my actions. His words kept ringing in my ears, "... *you'd do this to me, us, and God?*

Be...because of a child?'"

I realised my thoughtlessness. How could I destroy my marriage of over two years over my desire for a child and condition the proof of God's love and loyalty for me, on his provision of a child?

I repented of my mistakes, knew God had forgiven me but wasn't sure he'd give me another chance. However, after making peace with God.

I knew what to do. I had to make peace with my husband too. Nevertheless, I was worried as to what his reaction would be. Would he still accept me or reject me? No, I couldn't face him, not with the gravity of my offence. In the end, I gathered courage and put a call across to him.

It kept ringing but he never picked it. I must have called him more than a hundred times, neither did he call back. And as each month rolled by, I became more desperate. It seemed to me I had lost Timi forever. Even after visiting what used to be our home and his office, the gatemen wouldn't let me in saying he was not around, and he still didn't reach out to acknowledge my efforts.

Except one time I scurried past the gateman and kept shouting Timi, I know you can hear me.

"I'm sorry."

The gateman ran after me, but it was not without a struggle. I sat on the ground fighting with him all the way and as he about to bundle me out of the house, I heard Timi's calm voice.

"Leave her."

Relief flooded my heart. But I also heard a female voice say: *"Babe?"* Like she was questioning his words.

My head lifted and I got a bone chilling surprise. It was the lady I had paid to set up my husband. What was she doing in my house?

I lunged at her like a mad woman.

"Sholape! What are you going with my husband?"

Her eyes flashed like dagger ready for a fight. But I stopped right in my track when my husband pulled her close to his side and spoke.

"We are now together. Wasn't this what you wanted?"

I wanted the ground to open and swallow me.

"Timi, my Timi is with another woman?" I murmured, cleaning my eyes to wipe the illusion before me. I must be running mad. There was no better explanation. I couldn't breathe for a few seconds and was suddenly enveloped by a chilling cold. I knew I had lost, and it didn't feel good.

If someone had told me this, I swear I wouldn't believe it. How could I? Timi loved me too much to let me go. I knew that as well as the lines on my palms. I had taken his love for granted.

★★★

I glanced at the radio still playing softly in the

background. King Sunny Ade's lyrics had given way to another artist singing the national anthem and the words jumped at me with vigour and hope - "Arise, oh compatriot."

"Arise, oh compatriot," I kept repeating, rousing.

Timi had made it clear that he was done with our marriage. To affirm that he wasn't joking, he even sent me divorce papers which laid on the dressing table too. But I wasn't going to sign it. Not in this lifetime.

Instantly, I knew what to do. I needed to arise and fight for my marriage. If he wasn't married to her yet, I could still win my husband back. Loyalty in marriage isn't one sided. I had to prove to my husband that I'd be loyal to him and that involved letting him know I'm sorry and would stick to him till eternity regardless of our childlessness.

If I wanted to see him, I'd have to attend our mutual church whilst still together. I honestly hoped that the weight of hope the Nigerian Independence Day and national anthem gave would reflect in my love and I could celebrate subsequent ones without pain.

If Timi wasn't willing to see me, I would confess my wrongdoings to our Pastor. Timi highly respected him and wouldn't disobey him. I wanted my husband back and would go to any honourable length to see us get back together.

I got up from the bed, walked towards the window and parted the curtains to reveal the bustling city of

Lagos. My eyes darted to the hotel's compound, it was a mixture of colours and sounds as many trooped into the lobby finding their way to the concert organized by *Basket Mouth* in celebration of Independence Day.

I felt a fleeting pang quickly replaced by hope, love and a sense of loyalty towards my husband. Quickly, I dressed and made a quick dash to the bus stop. I was at the bus stop before I remembered to order a ride on Uber app. In ten minutes, I was on my way to Word of Life Bible Church.

My breath caught as I spotted him at the front row seat, his head was slightly bent, deeply immersed in prayer. There was a service ongoing. My eyes misted. Oh! How I missed my husband. I couldn't wait to wrap my hands around him and rest my head on his chest.

After the service, he was nowhere to be found. I strained my neck searching for him among the throngs of believers in the church building. Luckily for me, I saw him walking towards his car. I jumped to my feet and hastened my steps towards him.

With muted breath, counting from one to ten, I knocked on his tinted car window. It took forever for him to wind down the window. Upon sighting me, he couldn't help but gape at me. I burst into tears.

"Why are you here?" he asked barely above a whisper.

"I miss you; I miss us, and I want to tell you that I'm so sorry. I was so foolish. Now, I realise this."

He unlocked the passenger door.

"Come inside."

As soon as I got in, he wrapped me in his arms and planted a kiss on my lips.

"I missed you too."

"I can't believe you've forgiven me and that you still love me."

Timi smiled. "Did you really think you could easily get rid of me just like that? I'm committed to making this marriage work. Since marriage has bound us, I remain loyal to you and even you can't thwart that."

"What about Sholape?" I asked, teary-eyed.

"It was a farce. She came around that day to beg for my love but then, when you came, I didn't feel convinced that you understood the gravity of what you had done. I believed you had taken my love for granted and I needed to make you realise this. I honestly was scared you wouldn't return. But I couldn't force you if you didn't want me. So, I waited till you came."

"I love you, Timi."

"I love you, Sade."

And so, we continued our journey hand in hand. Our love shone like the sun, proof of the love and loyalty we had towards each other regardless of the challenges we kept facing.

The story still doesn't end here. Exactly a year later, miraculously, I had my first child. We named him Ilerioluwakonilolaise.

Olayemi Oyin is a Nigerian writer with a deep passion for exploring identity, social issues, and romance through her storytelling. She is the author of *Broken*, *Untamed*, *Finding Mr. Right*, and *Colours of Grace* - each weaving together themes of love, resilience, and self-discovery.

Outside of writing, Olayemi is an enthusiastic lover of art, music, and culture, a self-proclaimed movie buff.

Mother'd My Girls

Chibuike Agbalokwu

The night was silenced by the immense darkness; the moon had found its way to its lover's bed leaving the night in the hand of nothing, not even the wind. I wasn't sure what woke me up – my dream or the hot night. I was sweating terribly.

I used my wrapper, which was loosely held to my body, to wipe my forehead. I contemplated throwing the wrapper away, but my last child will always remind me of her presence in the room. She would turn and sleep-talk, beckoning on her sleep friends. Most of what she says eludes me. Not only that, but I would also be a feast to the whining mosquitoes. Else, I would have thrown away the mosquito net too. The nets felt like fiery confinement inside my already small apartment.

A dog barked from a distance continuously. The bark heralded the loud screech coming from a machete being scratched against a hard surface. It came suddenly and it startled me. I knew it was the local vigilante guarding the street, but I never got used to their noise. Even though they had been around for years and had continuously disturbed our night with either the machete, the whistle, or their chants. We pay through our nose for us to sleep peacefully but we have only gotten nuisance. The noise was an assurance to other residents but never to me.

"What is it?" my husband asked in a calm throaty voice. I jumped. I didn't know he was awake.

"Chi'm," I exclaimed. I had to hold my chest with my hand to steady my heart which was racing. I had sat up on the bed. "I wake you? Sorry."

"I don wake for the past thirty minutes. You are turning again in bed, pushing and kicking like sey you get bad dream."

His voice was lovely and calm. I couldn't trace any sign of anger and it was greatly fulfilling. It was an assurance that he still loved me. I wiped my face again with my wrapper thinking of what to say.

"You were calling Chioma again and again," he said.

My response was a series of stuttered incoherent words, but I made sure to let him know it was not a dream but rather, the heat. He didn't respond to my gibberish but rather dragged me gently to lie down. He had heard that response a thousand and one times. He untied my wrapper and pulled it down to my waist.

I protested in my heart; our children might wake up anytime. He cladded me with his body. The worst thing that could happen this night was sex. I hadn't made up my mind to refuse yet, but he produced a hand fan and started fanning me. I gave a silent thanksgiving prayer. I couldn't believe I let him know the name of my last child. My last dead baby.

Chioma will always come to me in my dreams. One time, she would want to suckle at my breast, another time she would want me to cuddle her to sleep, other times she would just want to be around me. But she always comes crying and wouldn't stop until I gave in to her yearnings.

There were days, if not most of the days, I wouldn't want anything to do with her, but she would not go away. I might beat her or kick her, my poor little baby, but she would keep on coming back. Her scream drives me crazy. I rarely slept well. What kind of a baby would not let her mother know any rest? Sometimes, I wonder how it would have been had she lived.

The morning came with its refreshing air. The very few minutes after waking up that reminds one of sweet nature. Chills of heavenly dew and breath of eternal bliss just before reality sets in. I call it dawn of reality and mine creeps in the way a dirty water tints a clear one upon mixture. The usual frown beguiled my face. The type that always got Obinna to laugh.

My sweet husband. My love for him never diminished despite what he made me go through. In our early years, he would be there to kiss away my anguish. He will then make sweet promises to me about how our life will get better someday. How our girls will marry rich husbands and our boys will have enough to inherit. In his breath of roses and promises I would draw strength and joy to face yet another day.

Today, he was not there despite my drowning sorrow.

The dawn of reality came with a sudden nausea. Who does not have the horror of vomit? My stomach churned terribly. I ran out to the gutter outside and vomited. I hadn't eaten much last night and had little to throw up. It was mid-morning therefore most of our neighbours have gone out. I touched my neck to discover I was running temperature. I swallowed hard. My heart raced. The feeling was nostalgic, and I dreaded it. I never forgot any single day, nor did I forget all the atrocities I did to Chioma. I felt myself falling.

E gburu m Chioma oo! I killed Chioma! I killed my baby!

Strong arms grabbed me by the elbow. I had gone swindling almost falling into the big dirty gutter where all the dirty water from the bathrooms and kitchens in the compound pass through. It must have been Iya Ibeji. I couldn't care less but trusted the arm to lead me to safety. My landing was soft, and I guessed I was eased onto my bed. I fell asleep. Later on, I noticed my body was been wiped by a wet warm towel. I slept off again.

★★★

Chioma placed her head on my stomach. She was smiling. I touched her hair, she's already a year old and her entangled and unkept hair should be shaved off. She kept on smiling. She placed her hands over her mouth to hush me. She was peaceful unlike what she had always been. It was like she was listening to my stomach. Suddenly, she started screaming and hitting me. She dug her nails into my skin and scratched. The pain was splintering. For the first time, I hit her. The blow was so hard that she fell off, I feared I had hurt her, but it didn't deter her. She came running back to me. I was screaming as I was trying to push her off.

Iya Ibeji tried to hold me down as I fought her. It was mortifying when I discovered she was at the receiving end of my tantrums. Filled with shame I started sobbing. She consoled me. I know she was sure I took in again and her pity must have been from the fact that my last baby was stillborn. Nobody sympathized with a baby killer. She didn't know I killed my baby. The food she bought from my favourite joint was not able to go down my throat. I slept off again.

I woke up to the ululating children as they made their way into the house. I jumped to my feet. It felt like I had forgotten to breathe. I felt like a stranger in my own world. I hadn't done anything that day and the children would be hungry. Their father gives them money to sort themselves out in the morning. It's almost dark and I have no plans for dinner. My body felt terribly weak, but that wouldn't count for anything. My family must be served. I pushed our cranky door aside to head for the kitchen which was situated outside the building.

To my surprise, I saw my husband having a hushed conversation with Iya Ibeji. Looks like that type of conversation a son has with the mother-in-law that results in him divorcing his wife. Many questions crossed my mind. Iya Beji is not my mother-in-law, but she might as well be putting in words for her. Here, no one minds their business. Then again, had she faced her business, I might still be lying in my own vomit outside.

Obinna looked at me and smiled. They concluded the conversation and he approached me. Iya beji called out to me before heading to her room. Obinna placed his strong arms around me. I felt his warm strong arms. I perceived his perfume which was mixed with sweat. Just the right dose that drives me crazy. I fell into his arms. His love mattered to me.

"You shouldn't disturb yourself. We will buy mama-put for the night," he said.

"Excuse me," said Iyene, one of our neighbours. Obviously, we were blocking her path to the kitchen. I felt bad for displaying such affection where she can see us. It felt almost like a spite because she was yet to be married and she was well beyond the proper age. The thought amused me, for even though I felt bad for her, I might still bring it up next time we start quarrelling on who messed up the shared toilet.

We continued on our way back to our room holding hands. I am pregnant and it scared me. I guess that was the reason Chioma fought me after some moment of peace. I would still want my days of peace. I don't want the anxiety of not knowing if the baby would be a boy or a girl. The thought of what I might pass through made me want to convulse. I tried to keep it off my heart till I would have to go to the hospital.

With his hands gently patting my back and the sweetest of voice, he said, "It will surely be a boy."

My heart melted and I could taste my bile in my mouth. The horror he made me go through because he couldn't have a girl for his fifth child. Even the takeout food he bought from a fast-food joint did little to cheer me up. I felt downtrodden.

★★★

It started out as an argument. I was afraid he will ask me to leave his house after the hospital told me I will give birth to a girl. My mind would run into a frenzy anytime his mother called him. I lived in fear. He was the only son of his parents, and it was only customary he continued his lineage by giving birth to a son. I waited for him to drop the bombshell, but he never did.

That cold night, he whispered to my ears how he would want me to give him a son. He loved me terribly and would not let me go despite the advice from his mother and friends. He promised he would not humiliate me by going outside to another lady. I felt his love that night and we cried together.

However, he told me he cannot bear any more expense for a girl. We were feeding from hand to mouth already. He told me to do everything I can to get rid of the baby, or better still kill her in my stomach. The Ogbuefi foundation will see to my operation. They would not give in to abortion because it is illegal and even if they did, he won't have them risk spoiling my womb because I will still bear him a son.

I agreed to all he said because he iterated the fact that he still loved me. I had to do what I had to do to get rid of the baby. Hence, my horror began.

Early morning, I would line up with the agberos, hoodlums, in my street to take agbo, herbal medicine, mixed with gin. I would take more of it to the extent of intoxication. When the vendor raised her concern, I would lie and brag that I took it when I was pregnant with my four daughters, and they came out fine. My baby would shift uncomfortably but my heart was set on stone.

Was it my love for Obinna? Or the fact that I want to remain married? Or pure naivete? I cannot tell, but I cannot imagine a life without Obinna and a family. What will people say?

Intentionally, I would jump the stairs in front of our building. I did this when no one was looking. Being of great height, I always land with my hands to the ground. I would bear the terrible pain that would jolt to my waist. If I felt like this, I wondered how my baby had felt. I wept every night.

The grief wouldn't stop me from sleeping without a mosquito net. I had malaria drugs more than four times before I was due. The sickness made me so gloomy and pale. People will ask me the reason why I haven't been to the hospital, and I will lie that it had always been like this whenever I am pregnant.

Later on, my husband will bring back some concoction. He said that it will make sure all my efforts were not in vain. He assured me that this is the only way we both get what we want. He wouldn't want any quack doctor to spoil my womb in the name of abortion.

Obinna would kiss me on my neck before reminding me that I am the only one he wanted to bear his children. His love for me knew no bounds. He knew how to hypnotize me. I would hold him so tightly amidst pain and passion.

Even though the concoction might be causing an unknown amount of pain in my stomach, I had comfort. Most night, with my consent, he would slip inside me. To be truthful, nothing could ease my pain, both his presence made me believe I am suffering for a cause and that we are in it together.

The labour came in earlier than I expected. The pain was excruciating. I wept bitterly when I noticed because I was sure my baby was dead. At that point, I realised what I had done. I drowned myself in the pain as a sort of mortification, but nothing could make up for what I did to her. I wanted to name her Chioma. I don't know when I did, but that was what I called her. The doctor was so furious. He was right when he said I killed my child, but it wasn't carelessness, it was intentional.

I had been moody and angry ever since that day. I fought everybody that crossed me. The nights weren't any easier. Initially, it was all bliss with Chioma. She suckled my breast; I would wake up with a soaked cloth. It all went bad when I started to resent her, she would cry all through the night. Although I slept, I had no rest. It became worse now that I am pregnant.

***

The passer-by smiled at me as I sat alone on the long bench of the hospital. The maternity ward was the only part of a hospital where you get to experience joy. Nobody is dying, just humans happy to bring another angel into the world. Women with their protruding stomach and men with the food flasks, flowers, and love.

There I was, amidst so much happiness, but sad. No one knew I came to the hospital. No one needed to know that I have inquired about the sex of my baby. The nurse had smiled when she said it was a girl. Little did she know she was breaking bad news to me. My husband had been all love and affection, but this was the kind of news that could turn him into a monster. A sweet monster, nonetheless. I sobbed. The thought of murdering my baby again made me nauseous. I ran outside to the gutter and vomited.

That night, I cried all through. Obinna still made love to me when the kids slept off. He fell asleep immediately after he released. I slept too.

★★★

Chioma had a mean face. I pushed her away immediately I saw her. She struggled to reach me, scratching, and screaming. My slippers came handy. The beatings did not stop her from attacking me though. At some point, I was trying to prevent her from killing my baby. She was just a year old, when I flung her, she flew a great distance before hitting her head on the concrete floor. My heart sank to my stomach. The floor was soon dripping in her blood. I screamed to my wake.

No one woke up, or they were used to my commotion and wouldn't lose a night's sleep. The dream was gory, and the headache that visited me was splintering. I held my head and with a hushed, scared voice I iterated, "Chi m oo". I don't know if Chioma will cease to visit me now that I have murdered her the second time, but at that moment, I decided that I will not kill my children again. Come what may. I laid down again, but sleep didn't come. I remembered I am yet to eat. There was a plate of rice by my bed. I had hoped to eat it at midnight since I had no appetite that evening. I scooped a spoon, but it did not go down my throat. I am running away with my baby girls. If my family reject me, I will find elsewhere but never in the house of a murderer.

Obinna woke me up with kisses. He fumbled my breast and brushed my hips with his. The soft words he

spoke drizzled like early morning dew. I opened my mouth to tell him off but instead, I said:
"She's a girl."

The Bus Trip

Ifumi Ehigiator

"Wimpi, Wimpi, Mile three, Mile one," a dark-skinned man cried repeatedly, each time wiping sweat off his forehead, his voice cutting through roaring car engines ready to pounce when the light turned green, blaring horn at intervals from the halted cars while Ekori tried to ignore the spicy aroma of roasted and grilled chicken from the restaurant across the street which was blending with the odour of petrol from the fuel station dosed the atmosphere.

Ekori swiftly dodged an oncoming vehicle running at top speed and sighed with relief.

"Thunder fire you there, where you dey run go sef?" a gruff voice shouted.

"No mind am," a woman retorted, shaking her head. "Them for gather burn that 'im car, beat am well."

"What do you expect in a city with a number of new flyovers and dilapidated pedestrian bridges?" a man in a green French suit retorted.

"No be small thing oo," Ekori muttered as she placed her hands in the pockets of her combat navy-blue trousers and walked by the tower-high traffic lights. Her self-styled red dreadlocks rubbed their rough edges against her anthill-coloured skin as she tried to ignore the few strands that drove their way into her navy blue crop top.

She had errands to run, buy wool for her knitting projects and get back to Mile Three within the two-hour interval before her next lecture.

Knitting was a source of income that had served as her backup plan and lifesaver in diré times of need. She had two customers waiting for the latest creations and wasn't about to disappoint them – they were regulars. She had to work for a few years as well before she gained admission into Captain Elechi Amadi Polytechnic.

In a year's time, she will be in HND 2. She needed to ensure she finished what she started about six years ago. The eldest of the six children, with late father and a mother, a tailor, struggled to pay her fees. She was well aware of the responsibility ahead of her and knew what she had to do. She had her life planned out already.

First, she will get a job, then open an investment fund where she will invest her money. It will be wise to maintain her craft. She knew at some point she would be required to purchase a knitting machine. That didn't bother her.

"When we get there we will cross that bridge," her late father's words, her mantra.

She, like a handful of other pedestrians, boarded one of the mini buses parked by the right-hand side of the dualized expressway near a fuel station. Ekori fanned herself but it felt like she was fanning the flames of a fire. Except for the tyres, slide door, windows, seats and windscreens, the bus was an oven, heat radiating from the metal box.

"Conductor, na one fifty I get for Mile three oo," a mid-fortyish looking woman clad in an ankara butterfly gown called out to the dark-skinned man who was wiping sweat off his face once again.

"Wimpi, Wimpi, Mile three, Miles one," the conductor kept calling out to another pedestrian without uttering a word to the woman.

Hot air fumed of fragrances, and a slight mixture of sweat diffused in the bus. In no time, its patched leather seats were choked to maximum capacity by passengers. As the engine came alive, a fair-complexioned boy walked up to the conductor and grabbed him by the waist of his trousers.

"You never pay my moni o," the boy said.

"Na him make you come dey drag me?" the conductor asked, annoyed. "No try this nonsense again oo! Haahn! Wetin dey cause this kin thing na?"

"Ah, see this boy," the mid-fortyish woman said pointing at the boy, a sneer on her face.

The boy's white shirt had browned from days of wearing it without washing. His trousers were suspended somewhere between his waist and knees to reveal ash-coloured boxers with patches of brown and white. He smiled frantically, exposing his yellowed teeth, as he and the conductor moved to the corner to settle their differences.

"I remember am na. When him come from village. Small boy," a passenger said solemnly.

"Very fine that time oo. Him hair black well well,. No be now when him hair dey like dust," the mid-fortyish woman finished.

"Ehn now. Na fine boy but drugs don finish am now," another passenger explained.

"Na wa oo," a voice behind Ekoir sighed.

"Dem plenty for Rumigbo na. Some don sell

property for house, even carry rent give just for one smoke."

Ekori avoided these types of conversations and pursed her lips in futile resistance.

"Hia," the mid-fortyish woman exclaimed, ***shaking the bus.***

"And dia supplier no dey ever smoke that tin oo?" someone else chimed from the far back.

"Talk true?" the mid-fortyish woman asked in a louder voice.

"Before nko? Him go smoke am? Him own na to collect moni," the firm voice added.

The boy continued to mouth-tussle with the conductor on the other side of the road. Moments later, their bus, along with others roared to life again and the bus motioned towards the express slowly. The conductor jogged towards the bus after he settled the boy who happened to be a 'tax collector' at the bus stop.

Succeeding, he dangled unsteadily from the open door, shouting destinations and collecting fares. ***At intervals, as the bus zoomed past restaurants, shops, schools and banks and the sidewalks littered with people, the door creaked as though trying to close but it hit the conductor and stopped.***

"Kala dey?"

Ekori tried to bite her tongue from spewing her impatience as the bus stopped one more time. A man alighted after stretching towards the conductor with a hundred naira note in his right hand.

"Wimpi!"

"Chinda!"

"C. O. E.!"

"Any Mile three, Mile one here?" the conductor shouted outside and then inside the bus, spewing saliva on the mid-fortyish woman.

"Mile One," the mid-fortyish-looking woman indicated and the bus screeched to an abrupt halt.

She reached out to the conductor. As soon as he collected the money, he threw it.

"Ha ahn, conductor, wetin do the money?" the mid-fortyish-looking woman gestured to the ground where the naira notes lay scattered.

"Mile One na two hundred naira no be one fifty," the conductor spat.

"But I tell you say na wetin I get be this na," the mid-fortyish-looking woman persuaded.

"Madam no be me oh," the conductor retorted, shaking his head.

"Why you dey talk like dis naa, I no tell you?" the mid-fortyish-looking woman protested, eyeing him and turned to leave.

"Madam, my moni remain fifty naira for ya hand," the conductor shot back and grabbed the sleeves of the woman's gown and held onto it.

"Wetin dey worri dis conductor naa?" the mid-fortyish-looking woman looked about and sighed heavily as she attempted to release herself from the conductor's grip. The conductor pulled her sh even further, nearly ripping it.

"Abi me and you no dey d same kontri?" the conductor challenged.

"Conductor leave am ooh," a man cried out from inside the bus.

"I go pay oo. No drag am like that naa. Na pesin mama be that o," another passenger said, alighting from the bus to become a wedge between the woman and the conductor.

"She says she nor get am, leave her," another passenger murmured.

Three people had their hands stretched towards the conductor with fifty-naira note, he stood confused, not knowing whom to collect from.

"God don save you today," the conductor hissed and released the *sleeve of* the mid-fortyish-looking woman. ***The conductor collected the money from one of those with outstretched arms.***

"Una, thank you," the conductor mumbled, after collecting money from one of the outstretched arms.

"Hewu, na God go bless una oo," the mid-fortyish-looking woman smiled as she adjusted her dress and sauntered to the other side of the dual road.

"But guy make you sef take am easy na. How you go hold pesin mamá like that? Pesin wife," the man that alighted before Ekori did, murmured.

"Bros leave matter oo! Me sef I be pesin brother," the conductor retorted and the remaining passengers alighted.

Finally, at Mile Three bus stop, Ekori got off the vehicle and sighed with relief. She had things to do, a future to build. Like her father always said: "When we get there, we'll cross that bridge."

Ifumi Ehigiator is a Nigerian writer and poet. Her writing journey began with a love for reading, nurtured by her father's passion for books and library visits.

With qualifications in Communication and Education, Ifumi now teaches in an elementary school. Her work has appeared in *Potted Purple Magazine*, *Gratitude Journal*, *Poetry 365*, and *Spillwords*. She is also the author of *Age of the Sun*, a poetry collection.

When she isn't writing, Ifumi enjoys drawing, crafting, and sharing her creativity on social media.

The S. O. S.

Aninoritse Ejuliuwa

She called it, *Ajenirun*, this thing that was following him. She said his great-great-grandfather offended it, defied its orders and went into the arms of a ravishing woman who descended from a lineage with a much darker offence. She sprinkled and smeared what had the colour and consistency of talcum powder but smelt like rotten eggs on his palm, which she had seized in her ringed claws.

He gagged.
She cackled.

Goose pimples covered him. "It will not rest until it wastes you all completely," she eyeballed him, "and poverty is just one of its means." Then she smiled, a smile that stretched her reed-thin, coal-black mouth to an impossible extent.

"But I can help you."

Wind gushed in and rattled the cluster of tiny mirrors and cowries hanging from the stooped, ceiling-less, rusted zinc roofing.

"It is already upon you, but I like you. I will help you."

★★★

In the rickety bus where they sat crammed like sardines in a can, one of the stubby iron rods another passenger held at the back seat poked mercilessly into Kitan's back. No form of adjustment remedied it. The smell of sweat and desperate humanity hung thick. The traffic outside was locked and loaded.

Beside him, T-Boss's laughter matched the conductor's bus-stop announcements and curses for hoarseness. Kitan turned his face to the window, fighting the urge to bash him with one of those rods. The whole spiritualist thing had been T-Boss' idea.

Ajebo, this your suffer no just fit you, rárá. I know somebody wey go fit help your matter.

"Vulture's beak and heart," he said in between sputters. "Three-day-old tortoise egg!"

Kitan pinched him to lower his voice and glanced around the heads that bobbed and swung as they dipped in and out of potholes. "Sand from my father's compound in the village," he added that technical impossibility in a wry whisper.

More laughter. "She must really like you o! Others don't get anything that straight-forward on the list."

"She said I can bring seventy-k instead, and she'll get the items I can't find for me," Kitan forced through a clogged throat. The sum dizzied him. His account hadn't crawled above fifteen thousand naira in months.

The laughter abated. T-Boss fixed his bulging eyes on him and leaned closer than the bus squashed them. "Nobody's head will go for it, not so?"

***

Yelling had become second nature. How else could you prosper? Millions of people did it, just with different, more sophisticated mediums. For now, his voice was all he could afford.

It had vanished after the first week of the strange lifestyle, leaving him disgruntled with his chest and legs burning. It was how the guys in the area started to call him *Ajebo*. Now though, he could give orientations to others who were new to the business.

The mornings found him yelling, "Onigo Ode!" from street to street, buying plastic containers and used syringes from whoever had a stash to sell. It was hard that first time: returning to the plastic factory that had sacked him from his clerical work to sell the recycled materials. The afternoons found him yelling,

'Mile 2, Orile! Mile 2, Orile!', and whatever destinations the busses lined up by the road were headed until they filled up and left. The evenings found him yelling politics, football, and area matters in Yorùbá and Pidgin at *The Joint* with the other *alaye*s – an army of unconventional entrepreneurs who were veterans in the yelling business – with Alomo Bitters clutched in his hand, the gin preparing to burn a trail down his throat.

This sweltering evening, the talk flowed well. The transformer had blown up again, so nobody knew when the area would have electricity. The Igbo guys down the street were really looking for *wahala*, and wahala they would get.

Remember Tunde with the big, big grammar and k-legs? He don go London o, imagine!

The vigilantes caught the person stealing people's chickens at night and beat him black and blue.

So as they don ban okada, make we throway our bike, abi? God punish them! Premier League go mad this year, o!

There was also talk about some sort of virus that had a funny name he forgot as soon as he heard it.

Baba Gesinde smacked him on the back of his

head when he stared too long.

"Ṣo wa pa?" he yelled over the Fuji music blasting from the speakers, barring his yellowing teeth, the air thick with cigarette smoke and exhaustion. "You dey alright? You quiet today, o. Abi?" He glanced around their dozen odd groups for agreement. They obliged him. They had zeroed in on Kitan, fixed him their questioning stares. "No gist about Oga Ariyo?"

He was referring to Kitan's socialite boss, who lived in an Ikoyi duplex. It was his only job, twice weekly, that didn't involve yelling, just quiet nods, and relaying the area's political climate in polished English. He'd grabbed the opportunity, even if he would spend half the pay on transport back home. Ariyo was a strange man who had grown children all over the place that kept showing up, whom he kept introducing to his unsuspecting trophy wife as distant relatives. Waheed the gateman passed the gist of their commotion on to him. He passed it on to the guys.

Kitan shook his head. Nothing today. They muttered their disappointment. He gulped more Alomo.

Then he said, "Ejo, I go fit borrow money from una?"

★★★

He awoke with a strangled yelp that was drowned out by the clap of thunder, drenched in sweat, trembling.

In the dream – nightmare - he was back in the mansion with the voices, the poundings, the impassioned pleas, the senseless laughter, the resounding silence. He was poised over the WC, retching dry heaves. The usual hand was running unhurried strokes down his back. He had turned, ready to see her smiling, battered face, the face of the mistress turned wife, the face of his mother. He didn't.

It explained why his skin prickled and burned as the hand went. T-Boss' spiritualist stood, eyes glazed white, wizened claw suspended mid-air, mouth hanging so low it brushed the marble floor. "*Ajeeniruuun!*" came her curdling hiss.

A flash of lightning lit the room before plunging it back into pitch darkness. Outside, the crashing rain held the promise of a strenuous, flooded following day. He couldn't go back to sleep, so he lay there, steadying his racing heart, calculating, one arm plopped beneath his head, the other fending off the mosquitoes that made it past the netting and buzzed around little Grace, who stuck to him like glue, and Morayo, who released choppy snores.

Her rounded belly jutted into him, warm with life. She was all glorious curves and demure mannerisms those years ago when service to the broken and abused women at the SOS Foundation had thrust them together. These days, she was angular and spitfire, her quiet strength mutating into fierce resolve. Those days, he couldn't wait to see her, to lose himself in her. These days, he just dreaded the sinking feeling of not having enough, of not *being* enough.

The fire she spat was hardly ever at him, though. She was his wife, his partner; he had her solidarity. It was the government that ran a system that would have an Accounting graduate like himself run odd jobs on the streets of Lagos, at the landlord of their Face-Me-I-Face-You one-room apartment with his garlic odour and drum stomach which only knows how to be collecting money when the house is falling apart; at that yeye Iya Sege who waited for me to start my fried yam business before starting her own just to frustrate me, but my God is still on the Throne; at the men whose mindless actions necessitated the creation of SOS.

These days, she stood at the window with her ingredient list and haggled prices with the passing hawkers until she checked them all off. If she had her way, she would storm the Iddo market and buy everything there.

KT, these road people will cut your throat if care is not taken!

But he couldn't stomach the thought of it, wouldn't risk her being jostled by the crowd. He would instead yell louder all day, every day.

Kitan couldn't breathe a word about the bizarre woman to Morayo. She would stare him down and ask if they were now begging on the streets if God was not alive.

He wasn't sure what his answer would be.

★★★

This time, Kitan heard the name of the virus properly, and it sank. Everyone concurred that it was too long, too fancy for something that promised darkness, and so, as the manner of mirth goes in Nigeria, it was dubbed *Coro.* News spread fast. The government announced a looming lockdown, during which everyone was meant to remain indoors 'until further notice,' which could mean anything.

At The Joint, the outrage was shared, opinions yelled, and humour inevitably conjured. Because in this life, you cannot frown forever. You just had to laugh at some point, or the grave would be much closer.

"*Irọ!* Fat lie! I no believe am. They just wan make life hard for people."

"How Oyinbo matter come take concern us, now? Why government go lock down everywhere? Abi na joke?"

"They say make we buy food keep for house."

"Ehh eh?" raised brows, incredulous smiles. "Them wan dash us the money, ni?"

"They say *Coro* dey kill plenty people for abroad o."

"Abeg o, *abeg!* I take God beg the people wey dey there. Make them stay put o. Make them no carry am reach this side. We no just want more wahala."

"*Joor!* If them like, make them come. *Coro* no get levels where we dey. E no fit kill us." Everybody agreed with that one and cheered to it.

"Wo, that one no kuku concern me. Na my business I dey think." This was Kitan's view. Laughter and conversation pumped heartily for a while before they began to peter out.

Because slowly, the grim reality that faced them began to set in. Talk receded to whispered concerns, to slow and deliberate sipping from beer bottles, slow and deliberate contemplations. A lockdown meant many things: no chance to yell and hustle, no chance to gather, for anything at all. The guarantee of sustenance hung thin.

For Kitan, the list stretched a gut-wrenchingly further. Morayo said the baby was due in five weeks.

★★★

Grace had developed a tiny mole on her nose. She gave them solid, looped soundtracks of all the poems and rhymes she'd learnt at school. Her days involved drilling them with questions about everything, measuring her height against the wall, rubbing her small palms over Morayo's taut belly, and exclaiming when a kick came, pulling the skin of his face and giggling at his exaggerated reactions, regaling them with zigzagging stories about her classmates and teachers, shuffling about the room, replacing this with that, '*redocorating*', playing *Suwe* with the other compound children. She was the unwitting inventor of myriad, merciful distractions, and Kitan loved her all the more for it.

Her four-year-old chatter was incessant. *Daddy, I'm sooo happy you're home. You will carry me on your neck, ṣhebi? Mommy cannot play like that again o. My friend Tumishe said her mommy used to eat raw onions when she was pregnant (*she would scrunch her nose and shudder*) Thank God mommy doesn't do that. Daddy, you look tired, are you not resting well? Daddy, I'm hungry.*

Time slowed to a maddening crawl. His insides in knots. The scanty palliatives of Indomie noodles sachets and twenty kilograms rice had been exhausted about a week ago, along with their savings and the money Baba Gesinde had lent him. Sneaking off to do whatever odd jobs presented themselves was getting increasingly difficult. Mama Ibinabo had given them as much credit sales as she could from her kiosk at the gate. They had accepted as much as shame would allow. Electricity had been thankfully restored, but it wouldn't be long before their bill expired, and they'd be back to square one.

From the thin wall separating their rooms, the voices of their neighbours, Akande and his wife

Vero were grating, each hurled word a barb that made Kitan wince, that made cold sweat break out over him. The nightmare kept coming, and even though he knew how it would play out, he still awoke trembling. It was suddenly unthinkable, handing over even five thousand naira to the wizened spiritualist near Ikorodu, *Ajenirun* or no *Ajenirun*.

If he sat still any longer, he would implode.

★★★

The operation was swift, the way T-Boss envisaged it would be. The man was a loaded deputy to the Local Government Chairman. He lived in Lekki phase 1.

When the door swung open, delicious cool air rushed at them. T-Boss shoved the gun in the help's face before she could speak a word. He kept his colourless smile on as they ushered the family of five and their staff to the centre of parlour.

"I hope you're not too concerned that we aren't wearing masks?" T-Boss' brows actually furrowed. "If you like, we could move over to your bathroom and wash our hands." Multiple heads shook fervently, *no problem at all.*

"Well, won't you ask us to sit? Where are your manners?" he said, transferring his mock incredulous expression from householder to householder. The pot-bellied man sputtered the forced courtesy.

Kitan kept glancing back at the door, ears trained for

sounds of trouble. His fingers trembled, kept squeezing and releasing the trigger of fake gun he held. His stomach gave a sickening pull. The other guys chuckled and sat. He followed suit. The lush leather couch felt like a caress.

"Your manners are bad o, *o ti bajẹ patapata*," T-Boss shook his head, lips down-turned. "Won't you offer us food? Do I have to tell you people everything?" After which they produced amala with peppery, meat-riddled *Efọ Riro* soup, which the gang wolfed down in minutes. Kitan withdrew a nylon bag from his pocket and emptied his plate into it.

T-Boss had the man of the house heft a black polythene bag into the parlour. The crisp scent of currency circulated fast. T-Boss grinned. On their plasma TV, a blond CNN newscaster with a fancy British accent continued on about staggering death tolls and stimulus packages, about Work From Home and mental health.

"You people have jollof, for take-away?"

They did. They were equally generous with the surplus raw rice in their store. As they left, Kitan balanced the weight of his package under his arm. He would tell Morayo and the women at SOS it was palliative from Oga Ariyo.

★★★

Everything was going so well this third time. He used the back streets, the cover of dusk, and knowledge from his first two woeful attempts to make his way past the military checkpoints and the black Toyota Hiluxes that patrolled the area.

After fighting irrepressible concerns, growling stomachs, Morayo's crankiness – which he preferred to her silence – and cracking numerous dry jokes for days on end, he threw on a shirt and jeans and hit the road. He'd wasted too much time already. These spiritualists were all strange ways and biting repercussions. He couldn't deal with any of that, not on top of what he had on his plate.

His share of the Lekki loot was thirty thousand. There was no way on earth he would hand all of it over, just like that. He tried calling T-Boss to ask if she would accept 10k for now. He would know since he'd done business with her before, but the Glo operator kept repeating all sorts of things: *The number you're calling is busy, try later, goodbye; the number you're calling is out of cell coverage, please try again later; the number you're calling does not exist, please check the number and dial again.* Finally, there were no more words; just a single terminating beep.

So Kitan decided to chance it. One more day watching his family suffer would surely off him. He spent hours mapping out routes, anticipating dangers and ways out, evading Morayo's queries about what he was up to. Struggling not to implode.

"KT, KT," she paced as much as their cramped self-con would allow, shaking her head, supporting her waist, pulling on an earlobe. "Oluwakitan Joshua Adetade! How many times did I call you?" Grace kept glancing up from her position on the floor and the nightmare she was creating with crayons.

Morayo wagged a warning finger, voice tight with tears. They came too frequently these days.

"Whatever it is you're doing, stop it o! I'm telling you now. *Mi o fẹ wahala, o!* I smell trouble in this thing you're doing! Heh." She folded her slender arms over the great bulge of her belly. "Let nothing happen to you, o! Let nothing happen to you!"

She'd kept at the tirade until he was ready to leave. Kitan crushed her to himself as much as her belly would allow, pressed a kiss to her lips.

"*Mo,*" her name bubbled from a depth he didn't know existed, barely audible. His eyes burned, but not as fiercely as the sinking premonition in his chest. Morayo buried her face against his pounding heart for what felt like an eternity. It was one of those moments when their thoughts melded in that way he still did not understand. In her embrace, there was fear, pain and acceptance.

When he finally moved, she clutched the base of his shirt in her fist, voice now placating, like how she spoke when Grace was sick or upset "*Oya*, at least eat something. *Ejor*, please."

He'd swallowed a few balls of *eba* and *ewedu* soup to please her.

Now, he wished he didn't. Because, at the vicious bark and a loud, "Hey you!" The food raced up his throat and began a painful squirm for freedom.

The stocky SARS officer with the panting Rottweiler reached him at the intersection. The small market beside them sat eerily silent as darkness fell. "Who you be? Where you dey go?" he yelled for backup and jabbed a finger in Kitan's face.

"You just land for here? You no know say lockdown dey?"

Kitan tried to get the planned excuse out. It wasn't working. "*Soro soke, werey*! Will you open that your dirty mouth and speak louder?"

His four companions gathered round.

Kitan's heart pounded.

The leader's bloodshot eyes narrowed. "*Kini*? You dumb?"

Kitan shook his head no. He tried again. "I-I just w-w-wanted to reach t-the ph-pharmacy."

"Pharmacy? Who sick? Na you? You get Coro?"

"No, no, it's—"

"Baba, this guy dey give you lie chop! See as him leg dey shake like fish, now!" shouted another one.

They sized him up.

"Wetin dey the bag?"

Kitan's heart sank.

"Na money? Because I no trust the way wey you take dey hold am tight like say na your life, *rárá*. You thief am? Na operation you just dey return from?"

Kitan gulped and shook his head.

"Baba, e too dey obvious! This guy resemble thief, now! Look am wella," It was the same muscled instigator from before. "I sure say him dey do *G*, join. Trace am now, you go find laptop everywhere wey he dey use dupe people. No mind him baby face, o." Then to him, "*Oya*, submit that bag for search."

In an instant of terror-induced irrationality, Kitan turned and ran. It was the shortest chase ever. They pulled him to the ground.

"Baba, I tell you say this guy na scam. *You dey run?* Run go where, now? Imagine this guy, o! Imagine this guy!"

He started to beg. Wetness seeped into his shirt; he'd crashed into a muddy, refuse-lined puddle.

The first punch came. Then another. And then another.

★★★

In this new version of the dream, several fingers trailed down his back, ragged, biting. Turning, he found the man with the scar beside the spiritualist; the man with the cool gaze, with the moustache. The man Maami had remained fastened to until he offed her. His father's hand hovered in the air, then fell.

Kitan jerked awake, hit a bare body, earned himself curses and a sharp shove that sent waves of pain sliding down to his fingertips.

It had been worse that first day.

Other heads showed in the sickly yellow light of the single bulb that hung from the ceiling. The air was putrid with old sweat, rot, and forlorn humanity. Brushing bodies, coarse conversation, and sour unbelievable stories - it exceeded all the prison cell stereotypes he'd ever known. His meal for the past week had been half-cooked beans sprinkled with white garri. It was quite the update to his exciting CV.

His new friend Paluzo knew something about all sixteen inmates: who was really guilty and who was not, whose festering injury contributed to the stench, who was there permanently and who was due to be let out soon. The oddly plump, grey-haired man told him that he was on that last category: "Them need space to put more offenders. Your issue no bad like that."

The certainty of never seeing a person again that pushes one to loosen shields and pour out their soul pushed Kitan, and he left nothing out. Paluzo listened with the grim raptness of a psychologist and responded with a plethora of biting questions.

Wetin he do na terrible thing, but why not forgive

your papa and free your mind? This T-Boss guy wey carry you go meet the juju woman, him life better? He don establish? You think sey the 70k na once and for all? You think say she go stop at money? You get pikin, abi? What if she ask for your Grace? You never even reach 30 years, abi? All this energy you dey burn for this matter, why not burn am for one single hustle wey you get passion for?

★★★

He wept with Morayo after the trailer driver that gave him a free ride dropped him off. Grace cried too, clutching him harder than her mother.

There was another cry that stopped him cold: shrill, livid at having her attention shared with this strange, battered man. Kitan cradled her tiny body and wept more. The neighbours knocked to say *Modupe, Oluwa, thank God o!* Pastor Kayode laid hands on him and spoke in tongues.

After the lengthy confession, a tight-lipped Morayo set the stage for a DIY treatment session that had the old wounds throbbing afresh. Then she forced a tangy herbal mix down his throat.

Kitan drifted in and out of a weightless, dreamless sleep.

★★★

"That spiritualist? She don die o."

It sounded like a piece of information the diminutive man in greasy blue overalls thoroughly enjoyed sharing. After weeks of tentative easing, the lockdown was finally lifted. Several people stepped in with help and, miracle of miracles, they had gotten by.

"She don *kpeme*," the man repeated. "They say na Coro." He leaned closer to Kitan, who had blood roaring in his ears, and lowered his voice, matter-of-factly, "Me, I say na her juju chop her. She overdo. Very evil person."

Then he straightened and eyed Kitan.

"I hope say you no give am any money, sha?"

***

He sat on the stairs of the neatly plastered Pentecostal Church on the way home, drew in crisp air and completed his SOS.

It had begun that very day when an unfounded love had pulled him and Maami to Chief's mansion, deepened with the vicious abuse, grew in length over the long years of running, of trying to forget.

Somewhere within those quiet hours, as self-centredness cracked under the weight of sober reflection, he remembered countless others who were fighting all sorts of battles: the afraid; the hungry for food, for peace, for love; the broken by circumstance, by others, by pandemic, by themselves. Then there were the ones who weren't even aware they were broken.

Save Our Souls! From Mankind, With Much Heaviness.

God must really get truckloads of them per second, rendered both consciously and otherwise. Anyhow, he added his to the catalogue. Didn't people say He heard and did radical things about their conditions? What did he have to lose by trying? That was that. He had come, he had delivered the message.

He was a leaf when he left at sundown, light enough for the wind to carry him.

★★★

A gleaming black Mercedes stood in front of the compound. The man who leaned against it was speaking with Morayo, who was gesturing animatedly. She caught his confused gaze and stilled.

The man turned.

Kitan froze.

The man with the scar, with the cool gaze, with the moustache. The one who authored Maami's fate, the nightmares, the running, the heaviness.

The man had tears swimming in his eyes.

Aninoritse Ejuliuwa is a lover of inspiring words, whether in a book or a song. She believes that impactful storytelling bears the capacity for positive transformation and is one of the most potent tools for sharing the Creator's Love in a world in desperate need of healing.

She is currently a Development Economics Masters' student at Georg-August University, Göttingen, Germany. Aninoritse is passionate about contributing to a society where people possess the freedom and empowerment to excel in their unique paths. Behind the scenes, she is working on her debut novel.

Wildfire

Praise Abraham

As the glow of dawn lit the base of the Oyo hills, a dark sentinel, like a bad omen, his powerful, bat-like wings sprung from behind his shoulder blades, beating against the ether, causing him to bob up and down haphazardly and heavily clad in a dull, tarnished armour that reeked of sulphur and ash, hovered above the city. His grotesque form was invisible in the physical plane. His name, Airegin, the dark prince over the midwest territory of Nigeria.

His jaw clenched as his serpentine eyes in an

unearthly green colour glowered with ancient malice at a particular location on the vast tropical terrain: Moyemi Heritage University - the most prestigious public university situated in the heart of the largest city of the Giant of Africa.

Airegin's lips curled in disdain. Nitwits! Especially the humans in this part of the globe. Irritated, he growled. What that one up there sees in them is a mystery.

Airegin's dark wings flapped impatiently, spreading wispy winds of chaos, and his lips twitched in an evil smirk. He raised proud shoulders, nodding in anticipation of an elevation to a more worthy cause of destruction when he'd please the evil lord with his next agenda. And as icing on the cake, spite the one up there and his meddling light sentinels.

In the Moyemi Heritage University, his prime candidate was Bisi, and his minions were ready to use her as bait to trigger a wildfire that would consume the entire nation.

His dark minions were ready. All their little mischiefs here and there were strategies that boil down to this present day. The flames of chaos would be kindled, not just on the campus, but on a much larger scale.

Let the games begin.

He spread his leathery wings and, with a thought, vanished.

★★★

With a heavy thud that resounded through the hall, Bisi Alege, an undergraduate in the Department of Dramatic Arts, crumpled to the floor. She hit her plastic chair and sent it toppling down with her. She lay motionless on the ground, her right arm twisted at an unnatural angle.

Her coursemates who had been standing around her raised an alarm. The entire class of over a hundred bored-to-death students, who were fanning themselves with their handouts to reduce the scourge of the sweltering heat, turned to the back to have a glimpse of the ruckus that had been made.

"Will you keep your dirty mouths shut? If you want to disrupt my class, then walk out the door and risk a zero for your semester test!" a paunchy man on the wooden podium barked.

The man was their History and Culture (HAC101) lecturer and a real pain in the ass. He'd asked them all to remain standing as they'd arrived five minutes late to his class because there was a big distance between this lecture hall and where they'd had their previous lecture.

The course was a mandatory one for all year one students. Many chose to 'stab' it because it was a waste of time to just watch the man shouting and trying to act strict instead of teaching. But the thing was, the man's brain could spark at times and he'd just do an impromptu test that would have a major effect on their GP.

"Sir," Isioma, Bisi's best friend, who had already slid down and placed Bisi's head on her lap, cried in panic. "My friend fainted and needs help. Her breathing is shallow, and her temperature has spiked."

The other students murmured worriedly like bees. The lecturer harshly hushed the class to silence with his Medusa glare. Everyone knew the HAC101 lecturer was a full-blown sadist, but no one knew the degree of his inhumaneness had made him so unfeeling even to another person's predicament.

"Then, carry her out!" he ordered coldly. "And stop disturbing my class!"

Idris, another friend of Bisi's, carried her in his arms. He'd lived most of his life in the north, helping his father's groundnut business and was accustomed to carrying heavy loads.

It was a good thing Bisi had worn a trouser that prevented her thighs from being on public display.

As they, the whole team of about ten concerned friends who cared for Bisi, hurried to the door, the lecturer shouted. They froze.

"Hey, hey, hey! Where are you all going? Oooo! So you think you all can use this as an avenue to leave my class, abi? Never! This is my domain, and you do what I say. Only one person leaves with the sick lady. And that's final!"

Isioma huffed, on the verge of angry tears, hissed and urged the crew on.

As they left, she could hear the bossy voice of the man asking all the students to write their names in an attendance he'd just begun passing around. To hell with his attendance, she thought.

They plodded to the exit of the class and trotted out to the main street as fast as they could.

Isioma kept crying and praying under her breath.

"Bisi, please be fine. Oh God, let her be fine."

Just as they got to the unusually bare street, they simultaneously were hit with the realisation that the transportation association on campus had protested due to the government's lifting of the petrol price subsidy. That was why there was no bus, taxi or motorcycle in sight.

Even if any happened to miraculously appear against all odds, there was a high chance that the driver would take advantage of their desperation and haste to extort them of their limited funds.

"It's pointless to stand here waiting. We have to get going!" Idris said, his hands burning under the weight of the unconscious Bisi he was carrying.

As they all ran, Isioma's mind replayed what had happened that morning. She lived in the same hostel, Benique Hall, as Bisi, but in separate rooms.

Yesternight, Bisi had insisted on doing a vigil to cover up her reading material. She didn't eat last night.

Isioma was aware of her friend's allergies to some foods. Which was why Bisi had chosen to ditch the cafeteria's meals. And she wasn't good or keen at cooking.

Isioma had volunteered to cook noodles for her friend, but Bisi had refused, saying she was sick of that staple fast food already. And so, despite her insistence, Bisi had taken only half a loaf of bread and drank lots of coffee.

Isioma blamed herself. She was a terrible friend. Why hadn't she forced Bisi to eat something substantial, especially since she knew how weak her friend's health was?

After what seemed like an eternity, the hurrying bunch finally arrived at the university's infirmary.

Bored-looking nurses lounged at the reception desk. One was filing her nail and chewing bubble gum. The other was watching a comedy on her phone and cackling like she was high on laughing gas.

Isioma knew the drill. The university infirmary nurses were renowned for their crankiness and irritability. Now wasn't the time for their drama. Please.

"Ma!" Isioma wheezed as she slammed her hands on the desk to grab their attention. "There's an emergency! My friend collapsed in the class, and we've rushed her here!"

She pointed to the bench where Idris had already laid Bisi's limp body. From the alarmed look on his face, it was easy to tell that Bisi's breathing was getting shallower and more laboured.

"Okay. Is she with her health care card?" the first nurse asked, looking at her with blank eyes.

"No. No, ma! We came over as soon as she fainted. I know she has her card in her bag, but we forgot it in our haste."

"Well, then, I'm sorry, but we can do nothing."

"What? My friend is dying, and you say you can do nothing!" Isioma was on the verge of screaming. "What kind of people are these? We're talking about human life here."

"Yes, I know. But that's the procedure."

"Besides, Nurse Emily," the first nurse said – Isioma hated her nonchalant tone with passion already – "Have you told them that the doctors are on strike? We cannot do anything except set a line for her and give her bed rest."

"What?" Isioma whisper-shouted in exasperation.

At that moment, Bisi's body suddenly stiffened where she was lying on the bench. She began twitching and trashing. The students around her began to shout in panic. Some, especially Idris, tried to hold her down to keep her from hurting herself.

Bisi's eyes rolled to the back of her head. Traces of foam began to bubble from the corners of her mouth.

"No, please! I beg you. Someone do something. She's the only friend I have!" Isioma cried, her mind reeling.

The nicer nurse, the one called Nurse Emily, sighed and got up.

"Bring her here."

After the nurse gave her a shot to calm her down, they managed to place her on a trolley bed. The nurse wheeled her into the Emergency Room while the second nurse tried to contact a doctor.

★★★

Tod, a light sentinel, the feathers of golden wings vibrating as if to expand the soft ethereal glow that surrounded him. He stood some distance away from the entrance of the hospital that Bisi had been whisked into.

He almost smirked as the light in him pulsed stronger when the atmosphere changed. He slanted his head, his eyes narrowed as a host of dark sentinels whispered discouragements to the nurses, telling them they could not break professional protocol and go ahead to administer treatment to Bisi.

When the nurses and their unseen parasites left, Tod glided without effort towards Bisi's room, her aura guiding him. He hadn't been given any instructions concerning her, but he, being who he was, spread his wings like a canopy over her bed, making it hard for the dark sentinels to send negative thoughts her way.

Bisi's life was slipping away, and no other treatment had been given to help her. He observed her with kind eyes.

If it was time to bring her home, he'd be honoured to take her into the presence of the One Up High. Even though it was aggravating that he had received no instruction from his captain as to whether to intervene, he knew his duty – serve.

Tod was honoured to be a guardian to a valiant soul like Bisi, who was no ordinary mortal; she was a warrior and an intercessor for the renewal of her broken land. Now, she would be crowned for her patience, courage and endurance. He prayed that the battles she'd won would earn her a reward beyond her imagination, as always.

He finally received a signal from his captain – a buzz in his inner being - and tuned in to the frequency of the captain's voice.

"Take her on a brief tour to see what shall be in the end. The people of this land need to be given one last warning. You shall accompany her before her release."

Tod's lip stretched slightly in a small smile. He nodded. Now, that was a much more worthy task to carry out than just standing here, doing nothing.

***

It had been six hours. So far, no doctor had shown up to take a look at Bisi. Isioma had called all the people she knew including Bisi's family members, her other roommates and the fellowship brethren.

Isioma had also posted on all her social handles that her friend was in critical condition and needed prayers. Tons of her over one hundred thousand followers had begun responding. Yes, there were perks to being a social media activist and influencer.

It was her passion, which explained why she'd chosen Law as her first choice. Too bad she'd been tossed to the Department of Social Psychology even though she had passed the cut-off mark for Law.

The two nurses they'd met on duty had left since their shift was over. A new set of nurses showed up, completely oblivious and indifferent to Bisi and what was happening to her. Based on the silent message they'd been projecting, they were just puppets in the system; it wasn't their fault.

***

It was when Isioma could bear it no longer that she remembered that she had an indirect connection to the Dean of student affairs. How could she have forgotten?

After close to an hour of making calls back and forth, a reluctant doctor sauntered in and took up Bisi's file. He announced that her case was critical—she needed emergency surgery—and referred her to the State's General Hospital.

The ambulance was delayed because of petrol scarcity. They had to rush her through the choking traffic and terrible potholes on the road. The general hospital was crowded, but somehow, they managed to line her up for a spare operating room.

The doctors began their work in haste. It was evident that Bisi was hanging on to life by a thread.

"Isi, maybe you should go get some food and rest. You look hungry and exhausted," Idris murmured.

Isioma hesitated.

They were both in the waiting room while the volunteer surgeons worked on Bisi. Idris knew if he watched Isioma take another frantic pace through the breadth of the waiting room, his resolve to be calm would break.

She stopped in her tracks and gave him a deathly glare that said: 'Do I look like I'm leaving here without getting answers?'

"Look, I know you're worried. I am too. But I believe Bisi will be just fine. She's being taken care of."

"I'm scared, Idris. She's frail and might not make it. What will I do then?"

Idris gulped and shook his head to assure himself nothing that bad would happen. He knew his world would be shattered if anything happened to Bisi.

He was in love with her, but he'd been doing his best to suppress it. Since the day she'd smilingly helped his confused self with his course registration, she'd been the only girl in his heart.

There were many reasons why he knew they could never end up together. She was a strong Christian; he was a Muslim by birth—not that he took the whole religion thing seriously. She was from the Yoruba tribe; he was from Jos.

He also suspected that the reason for her frail state of health was that she was a sickler. His was an AS genotype, meaning they were incompatible. Besides, his parents had done their duty years earlier to secure him an eligible damsel through betrothal. It was the way and culture of their tribe. Then, he'd been in JSS1 and the girl was in primary school.

As much as he kept reminding himself that Bisi was not the one for him, each time he looked at her and saw her infectious joy and zeal despite her condition, he saw a woman whose value could not be measured.

He wanted to protect her from the cruelty of the world. He wanted to make her safe. But all he was reduced to doing was love her from a distance, not certain if she even felt anything for him too.

★★★

"Bisi is a good girl. She never for once ceased to pray that Nigeria will be better. She had faith in a better Nigeria. And she even said she'd never be like others who were happy to *japa* from this country. Look what it's cost her now," Isioma said, breaking down in a fresh round of tears.

"Her dream is to influence people through the movies she'll act in and produce that there can be a better, God-governed Nigeria. She has to scale through this."

Two doctors in blue came out with stoic faces.

"Who are the parents of Miss Bisi Alege?" the lead surgeon asked, scanning the scanty waiting room.

"They're not here yet," Isioma said, hurrying to them, Idris in her wake. "They're on their way."

"Oh! Then I'm sorry I can't tell you anything."

Isioma frowned, her heart thudding as different possibilities ran through her mind.

As the lead surgeon turned to leave and attend to other duties, she grabbed his coat, stopping him, and looking at him through teary eyes.

"Doctor! See, I am her closest friend. I'm practically her blood sister. Tell me she's alright, or else I might die from apprehension."

The surgeon looked from the worried-faced Idris to Isioma. He wanted to tell the guy to take Isioma away from him, but he had a change of heart when he looked at her and saw her desperation.

He let out a whoosh of air.

"Well, I'm sorry. We did our best, but we lost her."

All Isioma could hear was a distant ringing sound as she stood frozen.

***

The governor watched his bald PA turn on the television with disinterest until he heard:

"*Breaking news!*"

"Increase it jaré!"

"*Bandits have ravaged the southern community of Ilesha, killing twenty people and causing property damage of over five million naira in worth. Their reason for such remains unknown...*"

The governor stared blankly at the TV for a minute. His fingers rapped on his large, burgundy office desk.

"Why would my little repertoire be punctuated by more bad news?" he grumbled. "To hell with their headache! If they didn't know how to protect themselves, that's their problem. I'm not God."

He hissed and changed the channel.

A young and attractive female reporter's face appeared on the screen. In the background were protesting students with placards and chanting. The scene piqued his interest. The governor frowned and listened.

"*About an hour ago, pandemonium broke out in Moyemi Heritage University. About one thousand angry students have taken to the road, as you can see. They are effectively blocking the Main Highway that links Moyemi Road, Oyo, to the Obayion Airport, bringing traffic to a standstill.*

We have gotten statements from some of the zealots of this protest. One Bisi Alege, an undergraduate of the department of Dramatic Arts, lost her life because, according to the aggrieved students, she was not quickly attended to due to some accumulating factors. The students are demanding to see the governor himself. They have so far refused to listen to any representative of the school authority.

This is Owodunni Shewa of Hourly Account News, speaking live from Moyemi Heritage University, Central Oyo."

The governor clapped his hands together in frustration as he watched the chaos on the television screen.

"What rubbish was this?" the governor bellowed at his personal assistant as if he was to blame.

"What's this mess I see? Call the military and clear off these pesky menaces from my road. I have to be in Abuja before noon."

"Right away, sir," his PA said, pushing his glasses up as he scurried out of the office.

***

Isioma's eyes were red. She'd cried for hours but couldn't still believe that her only friend was gone.

Being an influencer on campus, she'd pulled enough crowds of raging comrades who were tired of the state of things.

It was time for a big change. And it was they, the youths and leaders of tomorrow, who would begin that radical change. If gentle pleas wouldn't suffice for the school management and the Nigerian government at large, then, they'd do it the hard, bitter way.

Enough was enough!

Isioma had to do something to numb her pain and guilt. She refused to accept that she was blaming herself or revenge-thirsty. Bisi's death had only poured petrol on the embers of her radical nature.

★★★

Mewling demons flew like bats over the gathering, fuelling the hate and anger of the students.

"Make them thirsty for violence. That way, we can proceed to the next stage of our plan. This land is ours to rule," Airegin telepathically communicated to his minions.

★★★

The droning sound of the machines in the ER had Idris's head pounding. How could Bisi be gone so suddenly?

He had to brace up and prepare for when her wailing parents would come to claim her body. He could already picture how hysterical her mother would be when she arrived.

He stared at the pale face of his secret love. An unearthly serenity was there. His heart ached.

"How I wish I could see you one last time and tell you all I've been hiding. I love you. Oh, Bisi!" he whispered, tears pouring. He brought her cold and stiff hand to his face and wept.

"Just one more chance to hear her voice," he said, looking up.

Damn this country! he mused. Things were irreparably shattered. In every sphere, there was a big loophole: The crumbling education system, bad health care, terrorism and insecurity everywhere, and economic meltdown, to name a few.

The doctors had already left. Isioma had left too, in a daze of rage, about an hour ago. He'd been too shocked to move or even console anyone.

Now, looking up at the TV screen reporting the news, he saw a glimpse of Isioma leading a protest. She looked savage and war-thirsty. She had become a wounded lioness. He hoped this was the beginning of a revolution that would awaken Nigerians to speak up against the selfish and wicked authority that ruled with an iron fist.

He also wanted to join and seek vengeance for the avoidable death of his love, but he had doubts, and he was scared. Something about this whole saga was eerie and unnatural.

After having a good cry for some minutes, he wiped his tears and stared numbly at their entwined hands.

He felt something squeeze his hand. No, it was her hand.

Her hand? Corpses don't squeeze.

Was he hallucinating?

His tear-blotched eyes shot to her face. His eyes widened as he saw her fluttering eyelids. He wanted to scream in a mix of joy and fear, but he just sat there, petrified by what was happening.

"Idris!" Bisi called in her weak voice.

"Bi-bisi?" he stuttered. It was too good to be true.

"It's so glorious up there and so dark down here."

"You're awake! You're alive!" he exclaimed. "Wait, don't talk. Let me get the doctors..."

He made to leave but she held his hand tight and looked at him through pleading eyes.

"No, don't worry. I'll be leaving soon. There's no way I'll prefer staying in this hell to the paradise above. The Highest just gave me a chance to warn you. Promise me you'll tell Isioma and everyone else."

Tears welled in his eyes. He was in awe. Her God had heard his request. He was grateful, even if this was temporary, even if his desperation had made his mind play silly games.

"Bisi, I- I have to tell you something... I -"

"Shhh... I know." She gave him that angelic smile of hers.

"My heart warms at the knowledge of your affection despite our many differences. But your destiny is here. I've fulfilled mine."

She coughed. Idris patted her.

She continued, "Idris, don't blame God. Don't blame the government. That's not the solution."

"Only if the Kingdom of God is established in Nigeria will things have meaning. This country has rejected Him and chosen her own schemes. Now, the darkness is so thick and is about to swallow up everything, leaving desolation in its wake."

Her glazed eyes travelled to the TV that was hung up opposite her bed. She, with Idris, watched with concern as armed soldiers began to jump out of armoured tanks and vehicles and began to threaten the students who refused to budge, holding hands and chanting a chorus led by Isioma, her visage like flint.

Bisi looked on sympathetically while Idris stared at the television in horror as the soldiers opened fire and began shooting at the students. Everyone scattered. Screams filled the air.

Bullets poured out of the guns of the government. Innocent citizens fell in a pool of their own blood.

The camera that had been filming shook, distorting the view on screen, as the Hourly Account News crew ran for their lives. Soon, the live broadcast got disconnected.

Bisi turned her attention back to Idris.

"It has begun. The dark forces have set their plan in motion. Will saviours arise to stand in the gap and fight for Nigeria?" Bisi asked faintly, tears falling down her pale cheeks.

Idris shook his head in disagreement.

She touched Idris' hand. "The Highest would have

you take up the baton from me. Heed His call. Accept His love for you. It might be that you have been commissioned for such a time as this.

Also, tell Isi, for she also is to join this cause and will survive, that this war cannot be fought by physical strength or weapons..."

Bisi exhaled. Her spirit departed from her body.

Idris watched her hand slip out of his, and his body shook as tears poured not just from his eyes but also his heart, not knowing where to start. A million thoughts ran through his mind: maybe he should start by praying to the one Bisi had always intimately called *The Highest*.

★★★

Tod spread his large shimmering wings, ready to escort Bisi's soul through the pearly gates to meet his captain, her true King. His heart swelled with reverence as her soul left her body and spread itself on his outstretched arms. While he shielded Bisi, he spread light over Idris to shield him from the dark sentinels.

In a graceful motion, Tod's wings fluttered, stirring the air around him as he began to ascend. He simultaneously poured the oil of love and grace on Idris as he'd been instructed by the One Up High.

Barely had he flapped his wings before Idris cried:
"Save us, O Highest One!"

Praise Abraham, widely known as PeculiarPraise, is an emerging voice in speculative Christian fiction, presently studying architecture at the Obafemi Awolowo University in Nigeria. She believes that storytelling has the power to explore and bridge historical, present, and imaginative worlds.

When she's not crafting stories, you'll find her immersed in a book, designing, or spending time in the Secret Place with her invisible best friend.

Flappy Wings of Freedom

Adaeze Chinemelum Iloka

The clouds were dancing, and birds were chirping, their multicoloured wings the day Umeh was pardoned by the head of state in Ugani, Bende Region. A state pardon only came once in a while, and this one was a miracle - the type that made old people dance the *Nkwa*.

Umeh sat in despair with an overgrown beard and a chest so lean one could trace the skeletal bones on his shoulder. He heaved up and down and yawned lazily, waiting for the arrival of his quiet twin sister, Zulum.

Zulum was the anchor in his stormy, dark world. She was the calculative shoulder that carried his head. Perhaps because they were joined from birth, she understood him perfectly, but she had nothing in common with the temperamental, paranoid person he was. People used to say he was just like his father, Okeke Aguba, and he always vehemently denied the assumptions.

He often used to swear to himself that he'd never turn out to be the sly, condescending, wicked man his father was. He wanted nothing to do with him and his evil blood. He was aware his mother lay on a hospital bed, swollen and in pain; it hurt him that he couldn't be there; it hurt him that Zulum was the man he couldn't be for his family. A family he let down, a family he promised to protect. Sometimes, he thought back to what happened that fateful night, the night he made the biggest mistake of his life; he killed somebody. He might not have pulled the trigger but he drove someone who did, on his creaky, commercial Okada bike.

He sometimes replayed the events of that day and wished he could undo his mistake – turned down that customer or picked up someone else. Maybe if he had picked up the old woman at Abapo Junction, he'd have avoided the whole situation that now saw him sitting hungry in a federal prison, waiting for his twin to bring him the usual watery soup and fufu he had come to love and accept, crave even; it was nothing like the stale food they served in his smelly, congested prison.

★★★

Zulum walked slowly over crusty, dried leaves at that time of the day when the sun loved playing with colours. Sunset, she glanced around her and smiled at a butterfly perching on a dewy scent leaf branch and made to pick it up, but the evasive butterfly fluttered its wings and flew off demurely.

There were little rays of light around her, and she looked down the hill she had just trekked across and sighed; the federal prison was just two more streets ahead along dusty roads, kiosks clustered streets, and big police bumps. The Bende federal prison, Ugani, was just ahead; its highly Jericho-like solid, fenced walls stood tall; people often say the high-profile prison was both a blessing and a curse to the poor community. It was rumoured that many sons of Ugani land who challenged the government were rotting behind the solid walls with no help coming from anywhere; they were condemned cases.

She glanced around her lonely, gravel path filled with muddy puddles, gently sidestepped a huge stone, and kept walking briskly. Soon, she stepped into a little street that read, 'Western Morning Street,' and just like she always does, she smiled at the signpost; she always wondered why the colonialists, in a bid to civilize people maybe, would name a village street "Western Morning"; people who can't read or write.

Ugani land was one of the core oil-producing states in the country, yet so poor and dirty, utterly forgotten and left to rot. The government kept taking and taking its oil with no interest in compensating the town or developing it.

She walked into the busy, dimly lit street with dirty lamp posts and waved at the old woman with a rusty tray filled with roasted groundnut; she walked silently in deep thought. Occasionally, she'd raise her head and give out something she didn't even have, a smile here and there, and while she smiled, her heart broke just a little bit more, but she kept walking silently.

She was late, and she knew her twin brother's face would be etched with worries, but it really wasn't her fault. She sometimes wished Umeh was there beside her; she took care of everyone, but there was no one to take care of her. She was tired of being the nut that screwed everyone tight.

She walked towards a roadblock and waved at the pot-bellied policemen on duty to let her through. They were all familiar now; she was a regular visitor at the federal prison, and as she walked past the now-raised iron wedge, she thought of how to break the sad news of their mother's dismissal from the community hospital and how her cold body lay in the mortuary to her twin.

The hospital was worried about the increasing

COVID-19 pandemic outbreak in neighbouring communities and decided her poor mother, who lay helpless under the captivity of kidney cancer, was a lost case, and it would be best for her to be taken home and looked after by Zulum, who would visit the hospital every week to receive immune-boosting drugs.

She understood what they were trying to say; they were saying they could no longer take care of her mother, that all hope was lost, and she looked defeated. It didn't matter that her mother's lifeless body now lay in a mortuary and no one was there to console her, and it didn't matter that she woke up to her mother's cold body.

Zulum looked up at the gate that separated her brother from freedom and her heart began to race as her thoughts drifted to the sad reality she now had to share with Umeh. She had watched helplessly as their mother withered away, slowly devoured by illness, until the hospital, overwhelmed by the pandemic, had sent her home.

For once, she didn't have a solution, in comforting words or action and it made her tear up, but she firmly gripped her heart and the food flask the way she already learned to and walked into Bende Federal Prison. She walked past a slim police officer and greeted him calmly.

"Officer Tega, Good evening, oh."

The lanky officer waved at her expectantly and made

to tap her.

"Ah Zulum, how now? How body?"

She smiled and responded heartily, "I dey oh officer, I'm okay."

The officer beckoned her over with a wave of his hands.

"You know say you go dey wear face mask dey come here again if anything carry you come here next time, this pandemic don dey spread fast fast, police sef na human being," he berated her gently and insisted she wears one on her next visit to the prison yard again and playfully asked her if she brought kola or a little something for him and his fellow police officers and smiled knowingly.

Zulum handed him a small envelope and thanked him for allowing her to come in late.

"Officer, thank you, oh! Abeg, make I give Umeh food."

Another lanky officer with bushy hair and toothpick dangling out of his mouth in a little show-off manner told her to bring out the contents of the bag she was carrying; she gently opened the bag and brought out a metal flask filled with bitter leaf soup and showed the officer who smiled lazily at her.

"Zulu! Zulu! Na wa oh. This your brother dey enjoy oh. Oya come make we go waiting room make warden bring am," the lanky officer said and stepped aside to let her in.

She walked towards the waiting room with her bag and waited patiently for her brother, the creaking iron chair she sat echoing through the quiet room.

An elderly-looking woman with a badge that read: 'ASP ROSE IGBOKWE', walked into the waiting room and tapped her shoulders.

"Zu kedu? How're you? Please see me in my office before you leave; there's good news."

Zulum smiled politely at the woman whom she had grown fond of, grasped her rough palms in hers, and thanked her for allowing her in.

"Mummy, thank you, I'll come in before I leave."

***

ASP Rose Igbokwe walked out of the waiting room and patted Umeh, who was being escorted in by hefty wardens. She smiled at him and said:

"Umeh, see how you're shining; your God is alive, and you'll see the light of the day again."

As ASP Rose Igbokwe walked away, Umeh walked towards his sister with an unsure expression on his face and hugged her briefly, afraid of displaying any emotions or revealing how much he truly missed her; he had to be a man after all.

"Nwa kedu? How're you?" He liked to call her Nwa and held onto calling her that, his way of holding on to some semblance of normalcy.

Zulum smiled weakly and grasped his hands in hers.

She looked at him and noticed how bushy he looked; he was her once handsome twin, the one everyone loved because of his natural charm and finesse.

"You've not shaved in a while." It was a statement more than a question, and both of them were aware that he hadn't shaved, but she said it anyway so she wouldn't be tongue-tied. She rubbed his hands gently and asked him.

"What is ASP saying, go? What does she mean by what she said?" Zulum asked, worried.

"I'm as confused as you are, Zulum. How is Mama?"

Zulum paused and swallowed gently, avoiding his gaze. Sighing, she looked away as she murmured, "Mama is gone, Umeh. She is resting now. They sent us away from the hospital, can you imagine?" she said quickly and sighed. "They said they couldn't do anything anymore! The hospital is full because of the pandemic they said! They sent sick people home Umeh, people are dying! God have mercy." Her voice cracked a little, and at that moment, she allowed herself to be completely vulnerable.

Umeh watched Zulum cry, and his heart broke too; it broke for things that should have been; he swiped his thumb gently on her tear-stained cheeks and placed his hands on hers.

"Ozugo! Don't cry again," Umeh whispered through his pain. "You know she suffered enough and deserves to rest. Forgive me for letting you down. I should have been there for you! For mama! For the past four years, there's not a day that goes by that I don't regret that mistake!"

Zulum shook her head.

"I failed her," Umeh sighed.

"No, don't talk like that," Zulum said quickly and took his hand while wiping her tears.

"Look at me, Zulum, look at your brother! I'm here in chains because I made a costly mistake, Zulum I carried a thief on my bike and he shot a man! A man is dead and I have a hand in it! But I have hope, I know God is alive."

He held her hands and caressed her palms in a circular, soothing manner.

Zulum smiled, her only hope, her true hero. She glanced around, brought out the food flask and quickly opened it for him.

"Eat, I brought food. Eat before it gets cold."

Umeh hungrily picked up the flask and dipped his dirty hand in it and grabbed a chunk of fish from the watery bitterleaf soup and sucked on it, he ate silently while Zulum gazed at him adorably.

When he finished eating he wiped his dirty hands on his tattered prison trousers like he loved doing so the scent of the food clung to him for days, it was like having a piece of family with him. He asked her about his only uncle who visits sometimes with her and she laughed.

"Uncle Obi was locked outside the state border for days because of the travel ban by the Bende district governor. He went to buy some goods for his shop in the international market, and they locked him out. He said the scene he met at the border is one he'll never forget; so many people were locked out because they didn't know the borders would be closed without prior warning; a pregnant woman gave birth at the border! He sneaked into Bende in a bus filled with his goods and coco yam. You should see his skin."

Umeh bent his head and tried to force a weak smile on his face; he looked back at her and asked, "What about Mama? What do we do?"

Zulum reached out across his rough face, touched him, and said, " Mama will be buried tomorrow; Uncle Obi and I will arrange a little burial with Reverend Mmaduakor, don't worry, I'll be fine."

He looked at her and knew she was far from being okay. He shook his head and looked down. Two wardens walked in, tapped Umeh, and told him his time was up; he got up and walked away without a word, perhaps so he wouldn't break down in front of his sister.

Zulum left the prison after briefly talking with the kind ASP Rose Igbokwe, who informed her about her brother's state pardon. She remembered how she took a deep breath and clasped her hands when she heard it. Umeh was really going to be free? At first, she thought she was imagining things. She felt better knowing that the only person who could ever truly console her would be by her side. It gave her a different kind of strength and hope. She knew she was going to be alright now; she didn't even know she sang *Amazing Grace* until she got a grip on herself and burst into laughter. She laughed at how crazy she looked, crying, smiling and singing.

***

Umeh, now a free man, walked into the heavy downpour with Zulum tightly clasping his hands after signing all the necessary papers. They walked under the rain into the little shed where Uncle Obi parked his pickup van; they didn't seem to mind the rain and their drenched clothes; they kept looking at each other and smiling. When he finally spoke, twenty minutes into their long drive home, he said to his smiling sister.

"What was Mama like in her last days? Did she call my name?" Umeh finally sighed.

She observed him for some time before saying: "She always missed you, you know. She loves you so much, I feel her presence around us."

He looked away from her and swiped his wet cheeks, grateful for the rain and its ability to conceal his tears. He looked out the window of the pickup van and exhaled heavily at intervals as they drove through the sloppy, dusty road that led to his house, a house he still recognised; he truly took in his environment and realised nothing really changed in the four years he was away.

As the pickup drove into the unfenced, little house and parked beside a dwarf mango tree, Umeh let himself be washed with all the happy memories he'd had in that house and smiled, but then his heart took in all the sad moments he remembered in that same house so much so that after a much-revered silence, Umeh braced himself, turned to his sister who looked lost in thoughts and said to her…

"I want to see her grave. Take me to Mama."

A worried Zulum looked into his eyes as if to ask him if he was sure, he shook his head in affirmation and jumped down the van waiting for her to come down. She gathered the bags beside her and jumped down from the pickup van. She looked around the empty compound, glanced at her brother whose eyes were fixed on her and pointed towards the direction of a shallow grave beside a chicken pen and said….

"She's over there," Zulum said solemnly then shifted. "I'll be inside."

Zulum turned, walked towards a wooden door, unlocked it and walked inside. Uncle Obi who stood beside Umeh the whole time, soothingly tapped his back twice and walked in closely behind Zulum, they both seemed to understand that Umeh needed privacy to get some things off his chest and grieve privately.

Umeh stood still for a long while, unsure of whether to move forward or not; he took one step towards the direction of his mother's grave and stopped. He walked to the centre of the compound, yanked off a bunch of fresh proteas and arranged it properly. He then walked towards his mother's grave and fell on his knees. He gently dropped the flowers on her grave and slowly, hot tears fell from his eyes.

In that moment, he realised that everything he ever lost was not nearly as painful as the loss of his mother, he mourned his inability to do all the things he promised her. He didn't realise he dozed off until Zulum's gentle hands tapped him into consciousness, she extended her hands to him, lifted him up and they both walked into the small house silently.

Uncle Obi stood at the door with a metal lantern in his hand and when they approached the entrance of the house he said:

"Will you come to church tomorrow, Umeh? I know it's too early but the new Reverend is a breath of fresh air."

Umeh shook his head and said, "I'll go, if Mama was here I'd never miss church service, so I'll go." Umeh smiled and said, "It's good you think this way, Ugani land is under siege by the government and their foreign investment companies, and the whole community is in a mess, I'm sure the Reverend will pray for you and our community, I hope God touches these wicked leaders".

Umeh sat down, took a deep breath and replied, "It is sad that Ugani land is one of the most backward, marginalized communities in the country, yet we produce oil. We always argued about it in prison."

Zulum looked at both men and how engrossed they were in their conversation and smiled, she smiled because just like yesterday, she remembered walking along the security-infested road that led to the federal prison and how her brother now talked about the politics of her community as a free man. With a sigh, she glanced towards the sky and shook her head.

Uncle Obi left shortly after his conversation with Umeh, he picked them up at exactly six a.m. the next morning for church service at St Cyprian Anglican Church, Ugani.

Zulum was grateful for the transfer system of priests because everyone in the community was tired of hearing the old Reverend Uchenna go on and on about Ugani land and poverty, no need to state the obvious. She preferred the calculative, principled new Reverend Mmadukor, she was surprised however when her brother walked along the cement floor with six other men, towards the altar in the sparsely populated church when the Reverend called for volunteer delegates to speak for the community against the marginalization of the oil-producing region. She was so furious that she hardly even waited for church service to be dismissed properly before she dragged her amused brother to her uncle's van and heatedly asked him:

"What do you think you're doing, Umeh? You just got back from prison! Why do you even want to involve yourself in something like that? What is wrong with you?"

Umeh looked at her calmly, his eyes searching hers. "Why not? Is there anything wrong with a former prisoner engaging in developmental activities? This is a great opportunity for me to be useful and stand up for what is right."

Zulum scoffed, her anger flaring hotter. "You're a fool, Umeh! This? This is beyond development! There is a full-blown war between the government and our boys, they vandalized oil pipelines and the government is looking for scapegoats, before you involve yourself in something like this, ask questions! You're not going anywhere!"

Having said that, Zulum stormed off in search of her uncle whom she found having a chit-chat with some members of Anglican Men Fellowship and signalled him that they could leave.

The ride home was quiet and the atmosphere in their dusty little house remained the same, it seemed as though none wanted to give way to the other's will and their uncle knew not to intrude. Little wonder he walked away from them after parking his vehicle behind a hibiscus bush like he always did and walked into his compound to enjoy the spicy Sunday rice he knew was already waiting for him, courtesy of his ever-smiling wife.

Both siblings sat in their uncle's pickup, each refusing to look at the other until Zulum broke the silence and said to her deathly quiet brother, "So now you don't want to talk to me eh?"

He shook his head, got down from the car and said," Lock the door when you get down, give the key to Uncle and come into the house, we'll talk after we have eaten. No one bickers with Chizulum Nnadu on an empty stomach, you'll always have the last word so I better eat and have enough strength for the upcoming argument."

Zulum seethed at Umeh as he walked into his mother's compound, glancing around.

Umeh glanced around, remembering how old he and his twin were when his mother was chased away from their father's compound because he didn't fancy her anymore, it always marvelled him, the sheer wickedness against women and how his culture made it easy for men to further degrade and set themselves as superior and second to none in marriages. The tears on his mother's face as she walked into her father's house and was embraced by her only surviving brother Obi who went ahead to give her their mother's old house shaped him into the protective man he was; it made him resolve to always do everything in his power to love, protect and provide for his mother and twin.

And when he went to prison for a crime he didn't commit, his biggest regret was not being there for the two people he loved most in the world and now he is going to make it right. He will make himself useful to his community and family, he will rise as the mouthpiece of the Ugani community and use his education to fight for their rights. He will meet the government and speak to them about the invasion of their lands and how poorly they're being treated.

★★★

Umeh walked into the eerily quiet town hall in the centre of the community alongside the Reverend and six other men who equally volunteered to speak to the government officials who would be in the community to negotiate a peace pact between Ugani youths and the federal government. They heavily relied on him, who happened to be the most educated among them because of his mother's relentless efforts to give him and his twin a good life, and to speak to the government officials on behalf of the community.

He smiled to himself when he remembered how his sister sulked all day and sneaked into his room like she does all the time to sleep beside him, he loved that he was still her source of strength, that she was vulnerable enough to rely on him for protection.

Heavily armed vehicles halted in front of the town

hall, four men jumped off the government-owned vehicles and walked into the hall, the town representatives stood up to acknowledge their entrance and after exchanging pleasantries, the community youth leader presented white stained plastic chairs for them to sit on while security guards stood beside the men on suit with loaded guns.

It amused Umeh how these men came with security details armed with heavily loaded guns and sat on plastic chairs to address community representatives who sat opposite them on wooden benches. The irony of it all amused him, the people from the government were dressed in exquisite suits from the proceeds of oil taken from their lands, while the owners of the oil lands adorned worn-out shirts and hole-laden tee shirts with guns pointed in their direction.

How were they supposed to have a meaningful conversation? When the atmosphere was tense already, Umeh pondered.

He stood tall, his voice calm but carrying the defiant spirit he'd learned to conceal in prison. Exhaling deeply, he faced the government officials.

"Is there really any need to involve guns in what is supposed to be a peace pact dialogue? Oga federal government director of the oil-producing regions, Na so? Is this how we'll converse? With one party pointing guns towards the other who is obviously unarmed?"

The uncomfortable director who led the dialogue

team looked at Umeh, signalled his boys to step aside, adjusted his tight suit and began to speak.

"I applaud your courage young man," the director started and fell silent, adjusted his weight, cleared his throat and continued, "Ehhhh... what you said is true anyway ehn. I believe you all know me but I'll still introduce myself. I am Prof Chris Onebara and I am the federal government-appointed director of the oil-producing regions in Nigeria.

I believe you all know why we are here, but I'll still state the obvious, however, I must commend you all for heeding the call for this much-needed meeting. I believe you all know that pipeline vandalism is a serious crime and the federal government does not take it lightly and Ugani youths have sworn to always incur the wrath of the government upon themselves."

The representatives glanced at one another and murmured: "What is this man saying? Hian! Is this what they came to say to us?"

Umeh calmed everyone down and urged the director who looked flustered to speak. He cleared his throat and continued.

The director cleared his throat again. "Well, there's bound to be disagreements but I will continue anyway, the government hopes that we reach a consensus and see eye to eye on certain things. I believe you can speak now."

Umeh stood, signalled on the other representatives

to remain calm and began to speak.

"Oga director we have heard what you said. However, I beg to disagree with what you have said. Ugani land is an oil-producing community and for years we have suffered grave invasions from foreigners, water pollution, and bad industry practices that has led to massive oil spills on our land and different forms of degradation. The bulk of the crude oil is realised from our land yet we are so poor.

We are part of this nation's main source of revenue yet we belong to the ranks of the most backward, politically marginalized groups in the nation. We are in the minorities yet all the majorities are using the oil from our land to develop their lands to our own expense and detriment."

Umeh inhaled sharply to keep his hurt in check.

"Oga director. We say no! No! To oppression of Ugani land. We are only demanding what is rightfully ours. Let the government compensate us, we have suffered enough."

The little crowd that gathered and perched outside the hall cheered Umeh as the representatives in the hall stood and hugged him excitedly.

The director looked at Umeh with admiration, stood on his feet extended his hand for a handshake to Umeh and said to him:

"I hear them call you Umeh so I assume that is your name, I am impressed! In fact! Proud of you and how well you have spoken, you will hear from us soon as I will now take this message back to the federal government and I promise you all that something must be done for your needs to be met."

When Umeh lay on his bed that night, he closed his eyes and fought the tears that threatened to spill; he wished he could talk to his mother one more time, tell her how much he missed her, and have her listen to him speak.

There was a loud banging on the door the next morning. It startled Umeh and when the banging didn't stop, he walked into the kitchen with an iron torch, reached for his machete and walked quietly to the front door.

As soon as he heard his uncle's frantic voice, he quickly drew the bolt open and ushered him in.

"Ugani cult boys have vandalized the pipelines at Igado again, Umeh!"

Umeh squinted at his uncle who was waving his torch around, his face frantic, his voice barely above a whisper as he panted.

"I know what will follow next, a mass arrest and imprisonment of all able Ugani young men! Quick! Pack your bags. Wake your sister! We will leave right now for my maternal home in Zungeru, when the dust settles we'll return."

Umeh felt it first, anger! It slowly seeped across his

neck to every part of his body, he turned to his uncle.

"Uncle, I have nothing to be afraid of! My hands are clean! I will not run away like a coward, I'm going back to sleep! Let them come."

He walked into his room with his uncle on his heel, barking and yelling, "You're too stubborn, Umeh! Listen to me."

Umeh had made up his mind. When the federal troop came and took him away in handcuffs later in the day, he held up his head and walked into the black van.

Zulum stood at the door with a guarded look. She understood his reason to stand and fight for his rights.

A week later, Zulum visited Umeh to tell him the good news. The real culprits - the boys that vandalized the pipelines had been found. He'd also received a free bail order from the government.

Umeh was relieved; he'd had enough of the fat bullies he shared his tiny, bug-infested cell with. He realised, also in that moment that his life was a miracle and this time he'll work hard to fulfill every promise he ever made to himself and his loved ones.

He'll ride on the flappy wings of freedom and become a better man. For mama.

For Zulum.

Adaeze Chinemelum Iloka is a Nigerian writer, creative thinker, and public speaker. She is a graduate of the Ebonyi State University and curates a vibrant blog showcasing her freelance journalism, short stories, and insightful articles.

She is recognised for her distinct voice in fiction, earning her 4th place in the *Covid-19 in My City* competition.

Her debut novel will be out soon.

Children of Chukwu

Amara Ozokwelu

I walk around the compound, over the carpet formed by the fallen leaves of the mango tree, through the spread of the Ugwu leaves Nne had planted, till I see the black earth dotted by flowers aesthetically grown around the ground where Papa was lain eight years ago.

"I am now a warrior, Papa," I mutter under my breath, careful, lest anyone see me speaking to the air.

"I can now fight for you," I whisper, my hands gripping the dagger blessed by the gods at the celebration to kill all of my enemies.

The initiation of warriors had gone the way I had imagined, the aggressive dancing of the warriors punctuated with gunshots, their strong legs raising dusts as they threw their weights on the ground. The crowd of older men and women pressed together watching the procession with awe while the children tried to mimic the intricate dance steps throwing their legs and shaking their shoulders to the beat of the drums.

My heart swelled with pride when I was called one of the new warriors, proud to be one of the bare-chested teenage boys becoming men with skin stretched taut over muscles, rippling with strength, and impassive faces to show bravery and maturity.

The men of Nanka village were known for their heroics and tall, formidable statures and incredible fighting skills.

There was a proverb that said it was easier to throw a mountain to the ground than a Nanka warrior's back to touch the red ground, so I stood extra tall, stretching my back to make up for my shorter legs and feminine features that had almost made me unworthy of being a warrior.

I inflated my chest, raised my brows, and pinched my lips, my eyes darting through the crowds, taking in the combined look of shock from most men and women and admiration from the young girls at seeing me, a woman, become a warrior.

Everyone that stood around me towered over me

but I reminded myself how I had bested most of them in the rigorous training and games that qualified me as the first female Nanka warrior, so I made fists with my hands pushing all my fears and insecurity in the dark room, deep in the corner of my brain where I kept memories of the night, I watched papa hacked to death.

Agummadu, the leader, had stood in front of the new warriors, his black blade reflecting the sun each time he moved, flexing his hefty shoulders as he riled the crowds to a frenzy while he recited the slogan of the warriors

"Nanka Warriors!" Agummadu shouted.

"No mercy!" I replied, my high-pitched voice drowned by their baritones, but that did not stop me from shouting louder.

"Nanka warrioooorrrssss!"

"Kill all our enemiessss!" I screamed to match his tempo.

Agummadu had drawn six long cuts on my chest with his black blade, and as I bled, the village priest had said prayers, mopping my blood with a white cloth. The cuts that will turn to scars were proof that I had brought honour to my father's name and that one day, I would defeat my enemies and bring destruction and pain to the land of Ago.

I whisper again: "I can now fight for you, Papa." Before I return to the house, my head bowed with the weight of all the things that could have been.

★★★

Ago was a village without culture where there were no gods, a 'cursed place' Papa had called it countless times, shaking his head while rolling his shoulders and snapping his fingers as he told tales of their abominable acts; how the men in their village left the farm activities to the women while they laid on raffia mats doing nothing.

I wondered what Papa would think of me if he were alive, a woman warrior fighting with a blade. I wondered if he would have called it an abomination, like half the elders had called it, throwing spittle on the floor when I had volunteered for the training.

My father had called the abomination of Ago men an affront to the gods. "Chukwu had not created man to lazily lie in wait for their women to tend to them," papa had said, and this explained why the village was cursed, why the sky rarely blessed their lands with water.

The enmity between my village and Ago had existed for many years, even before my grandfather was born. My father had told me it all started when the King of Ago and his son visited the king of Nanka, my village, to ask for his only daughter's hand in marriage to foster the unity between the two villages.

The celebration of their marriage had gone on for

days, and the then king of Nanka, my king, had gifted the new couple the most fertile plot of land beside the river. It was considered a gesture that showed the bond the two villages now shared. An Igbo man never gave out his land. Lands were prized possessions, as the grounds tied you to your ancestors and should always be guarded from outsiders.

All was well until the new husband of the King's daughter sent her back to her father's house with tales of her promiscuity. She had called the name of another man while the prince was inside of her, their bodies singing old tunes of procreation. She was labelled *akwuna* – a lustful woman that seeks the pleasures of other men.

The marriage was over; a prince could never marry a lady whose body yearned for another man and whose body had a dangling tool between his legs.

A bride sent back to her father's home was a shame that burnt the ears and caused men to hide, shunning Umunna meetings till the news blew over, but to send home a king's daughter was an insult to the entire community. The community bristled with anger, even toddlers that filled their mouths with sand were inactive, as the entire community mourned their shame.

The tension multiplied after the suicide of the King's daughter, and the entire community screamed for vengeance resulted in a war that attributed to the loss of lives from both villages.

The two villages had burnt and bled till the royals agreed on a truce and the return of the gifted land as a sign of peace.

Many years have passed, and the gifted land was still the cause of chaos and bloodshed. Ago village, in a severe season of drought, had claimed the land as rightfully theirs, and the killings and unrest had continued, taking my father along with it.

I was consumed with the need to prove myself, to pay back in grief the debt I owed to the scared faces of Ago warriors.

★★★

"Those men should not be allowed to come into our village, talk more of dining with us when our women and children are present," Agummadu spat, reiterating his view on his displeasure of the oath cleansing ritual *iko mmee*.

"*Tufiakwa*! They want to dis-virgin and disgrace more of our women, *o kwa ya*. The king is too blind to see this," he continued as he mopped the beads of sweat on his face that was the colour of red dust glowering at the armed men of Ago village standing at the far side of the field.

I and the rest of the warriors have been assigned to ensure the peace of the oath cleansing ritual. The blood-soaked soil of our villages would be cleansed by the scooping away of the blood-sodden earth by the chief priests of both communities.

The ritual was done to usher in a new era of peace and puts a seal of agreement between the villages and their gods.

I watched the procession, observing the uneasiness of the kings at sharing a table with a lifelong enemy. A massive celebration would begin once the priests were done pouring libations on the ground and sacrificing the many livestock provided for the ritual.

The two priests worked in unison, their bald heads, red coverings, and dark tattoos were the only thing they had in common for my priest was as tall as a palm tree, rolling his head and hunched shoulders with every incantation that poured freely out of his lips while the priest of Ago was small and round his pot stomach an unusual attribute of those chosen by gods.

The peace ritual changed nothing about how I felt; my blade hungered for the blood of Ago men.

There was no scooping of Papa's blood and no burying of hatchets till the thing inside me that grew every day, feeding on my life force, sucking away all of my joy sank its teeth into the blood of Ago warriors and carved its name in history.

Time moved like a snail, each step of the ritual

dragging on for longer than I expected till I noticed him, my eyes locking with his. Most men shot daggers at me with their eyes or shamelessly leered at me, but his look was different. His eyes spoke lengthy words of awe and desire, and I did not want to look away.

The two long scars on both sides of his face made most Ago men resemble *ekwensu,* but it suited him perfectly. The dark scars, a colourful contrast to his skin, a rich yellow, the colour of overripe pawpaw and his long legs like the trunk of a coconut tree made me give him the name Anyanwu, the god of the sun.

I watched him walk towards me, and I found myself walking to meet him halfway, my steps light with new purpose, the innate desire to know this man that bored holes into my mind till I am standing before him, the ritual forgotten; parallel would never meet.

"You are not allowed to look at me that way," I say, meeting his gaze, the blade in my hand unnaturally heavier.

"I thought we were here to broker peace," he replied, his full lips stretching into a toothless smile.

I clenched my jaws.

"In my village, women with front teeth that never meet are almost worshipped," he said, his face impassive. "It is considered the ultimate form of beauty for the gods to bless your teeth."

His voice was exactly like I thought it would be; it felt like drinking cold water gotten from a calabash on a sunny day. I search for words to say to avoid sounding like a young maiden meeting a man for the first time.

"I would like to know who cut you," he said, frowning at my chest

"Why?" I reply, my grip on my blade loosening. I had never felt so free with anyone, including my kin, and it bothered me this connection that felt like it had been formed in my past life.

"I would like to cut him to pieces for daring to draw lines on a skin this flawless, cocoa smeared with oil."

I tried hard to hide the smile on my face and the heartbeat that screamed in my ears.

"You do realise you're threatening my leader at a peace ritual, and this could cost you your head."

He looked away from me and watched the crowd "If this goes well, this war can finally be over."

"The ritual cannot bring the dead to life," I say, staring at him. I reminded myself that he was still the enemy. "It cannot bring food to the widows and orphans; your men have made."

"We have all lost someone in this war, Agu," he said solemnly, looking right into my eyes.

"Agu?" I ask.

"Well, I hear you fight like a lion," he replied with a small laugh that softened his features. I wished he would laugh more so I could see his full nose wrinkle again and his eyes disappear into their sockets.

I don't feel the need to defend myself, to let the thing inside my body embrace me like it did whenever I interacted with men, where every sentence was layered with mockery.

I sense his respect, evident in how he folded his hands behind him, so I smile, pushing the thing far into the corners of my mind. I feel the need to peel off the layers of covering and relax into the strange need of my body to be seen by him and to appreciate his god-like features. The loud noise from the ritual felt like it was miles away; it was just him and I standing under the full glare of the sun.

"Peace is a fragile thing," I say. "It is hard to lose people but even harder when their chi has not called them, and their life is brutally stolen from their body."

"We are all scared and bearing the weight of our pain, some more than others," he mumbled softly, pain etched in his face as he willed his eyes to meet mine while I stared into the crowd.

"What we choose to do with the pain is what matters," he continued. "I am sorry about the death of your father."

I wonder how he knows about papa, and I remember how the entire village had talked about his death, so I fight the urge to weep and rid myself of all the tears I never let free. I want him to stop talking about papa as I am too tired to retreat into my shell, so

I let him speak as I feel the first drop of tears fall from my eyes.

"I am sorry you had to watch him die," he said, his hands reaching for my palm.

I hear gunshots, the hastened movements of feet, the cry of a child, and the scream of a warrior in pain and know the ritual was over and chaos still lived in my land but I continue to lock eyes with him till he hits his blade with my blade; a sign of peace and understanding since the days of my ancestors, a sad smile on his face as he says" I guess, we can never be free."

I watch him disappear into the crowd, his blade clashing with the blade of my kin, as I swiftly draw the blood of a young Ago warrior, slicing open his stomach, and I know, I would never know the name of the man that looked like Anyanwu and made me feel whole. He, like me, was a child of Chukwu born into a world of hate.

Amara Ozokwelu was born in Lagos, Nigeria, where she developed a deep love for storytelling from an early age. She holds a bachelor's degree in microbiology and currently works as a quality control analyst at a leading FMCG company in Lagos.

Beyond professional pursuits, Amara enjoys watching movies and values engaging conversations.

Austin Tries to Do Better

Derek Ehiorobo

A day comes in every man's life when he wakes up thinking, 'I was made for more than this.' Ask him what 'this' is, and he will never be able to tell you.

That was me last week Monday, and is the reason I am at this symposium, adjusting this hungry python of a necktie, wound around my collar. I hate ties, but this feels like an appropriate event to wear one.

There is air conditioning, but I am sweating through my shirt, doing my best to look polite while trying to find a seat. I am at a place called The Hall of Impact, which I think is the most ridiculous name for anything I have ever heard.

There are rows of red cushioned chairs arranged in front of a raised platform. The hall is dimly lit, but I can make out the shapes of men and women in serious clothes greeting each other in firm handshakes.

I don't expect to see any familiar face here, so I pick a seat beside a huge man in a blue-striped suit. He looks at me and nods, and I nod back. I settle into my chair and take a deep breath, looking around once more.

Some dude in a black jacket is on the platform now, making sure the microphone is working and turning on the presentation screen. It flicks on and washes everyone with a bright blue light before switching to a bright, obnoxious poster that says, 'Shake off your limits and change your life,' in bold fonts.

***

The man beside me snorts, and I glance at him and see he is scrolling through videos on TikTok. I watch two beads of sweat race down his thick neck and diffuse on his collar. His suit jacket looks too small for him, with his button barely keeping his stomach in.

I notice we are wearing the same watch and roll up my sleeves.

I can start a conversation with this.

Why the hell do I even want to do that?

I roll my sleeves back down and wait for the event

to start. The lights in the hall go off, except the ones pointed at the platform.

It's like I'm watching the start of a stage play. A short man in a grey tee shirt and blue jeans climbs the stage, and everyone rises to give him a standing ovation.

His eyes look boisterous and intelligent, and his cheeks have deep dimples, they add to the energetic, youthful air he has, contrasted heavily by his receding hairline and silver facial hair.

He waits until the ovation stops and then grins confidently.

"I am so excited to be in the midst of future world changers," he says, and another round of applause follows.

I start thinking of all the things I could have bought with the money I paid to be here.

"You can have your seat," he says. "Now, let's talk impact."

***

As cynical as I usually am, that event did not feel like a waste of time. Matter of fact, I don't think I've ever felt this motivated.

I'm sitting on my bed, in my dingy one-room apartment as several wheels spin in my head. I look at the phone in my hand: I want to start an online business, write a script for my abandoned YouTube channel, call my crush and tell her I love her, apologize to my parents for being a disappointment, and delete all social media.

My heart is beating so fast that I fear I might pass out. My legs are shaking, full of energy. I think, 'I can do so much with my life. I should be doing so much with my life.'

I get up and make my bed.

I open my windows, pulling the curtain so I can have proper ventilation.

I pick up the broom leaning beside my mini fridge and start to sweep, enjoying the swing of my arm. Dust rises, and the light coming from the windows bathes each particle in a warm glow.

I cough and arrange my shoes, and eye the sneaker that's hanging by a thread, the pam-slippers that I've been meaning to fix for about six months now and sigh.

"To the trash you go," I say to both of them.

I pack all the dust and food wrappers, take off my sweat-soaked shirt, and sit on the floor, wondering what I'm going to do next with all this energy.

I can feel my phone pulling me towards it with a lasso, and I don't resist, I go to my phone and unlock it, ready to change my life forever.

The balding speaker at that event said something about how everything we see today came into being because someone out there in the world decided to take risks.

All my life, I've felt like a leaf, floating on a lazy

stream, with no idea where it's going or why. But today, I figure I can swim towards a crazy current and just have fun with it.

My fingers hover over my email app. I have 11 job applications and 2 competition entries gathering dust in my drafts. I puff my cheeks and click send on all of them.

It feels good in a way I cannot explain. I almost feel like a responsible adult, I can even picture myself finally getting an *I'm proud of you*, a handshake from my dad. I know I'd have to do more than send a few job applications to earn that, like find a cure for cancer, solve Nigeria's light issues or become my sister.

I'm going to continue riding this high for now. So, without giving it a single thought, I call one of my friends.

I wait, biting down my lower lip as her line rings until it cuts off. I'm glad she didn't pick up immediately. I would have panicked and abandoned the mission.

I call her again, going over what I want to tell her in my head. It's a jumbled mess of words but the main gist is that I've been in love with her for as long as I can remember.

She doesn't pick up this time either. I sit on my bed listening to the dull ringing, until it cuts off again. I sigh and drop my phone on the bed.

I decide to continue changing my life. I take off my

pants and enter my bathroom with only my boxers on, ready to finally scrub the mould off the old tiles.

It smells so damp and horrid, I get a change of heart and promise myself to get back to it on a day I feel even braver. Now, I can divert my attention to something else: my dirty laundry.

I open my wardrobe and a heap of messy clothes fall out and bury me. I fight my way out of it, barely making it out alive, and work to dump them all in a bag.

I hang the bag on my shoulder and take one look at my phone as I'm about to leave. I normally plug in my headphones and listen to music whenever I'm going anywhere, but the balding impact man mentioned something about weaning yourself off dependence on your phone, so I'm going to leave it on my bed.

I close the door and start my harrowing, phone-less journey to the laundromat. I have to cross several deserts, climb a frost-covered mountain, jump over a lava pit, and then. . . okay, the place is just 2 streets away from where I live, but it really did feel like this because the walk was too quiet.

One of the main talking points at the symposium was how people these days dread spending time with their thoughts, so we turn to distractions for easy gratification, instead of facing the uncomfortable quiet head-on.

I don't need anyone to tell me I hate spending time

with myself, especially when the voice in my head works round the clock to let me know how much I suck.

I guess now, I can try to think about other things. For example, there is a daycare here. I walk past the colourful signboard, whispering the names of every cartoon character I can recognise on its walls: Winnie the pooh, Bugs bunny, Sofia the first, Ben 10, Brandy and Mr Whiskers.

A strong wave of nostalgia hits me so hard, I almost fall on my knees crying. I keep walking anyway. I can vaguely remember when that building was still in development: its ugly, naked brick walls, no roof, heaps of sand and gravel on one corner waiting to be used.

It feels weird. This building has been finished, painted, given a purpose, and I have been trapped in time. Moving in the same loop like a tireless hamster, playing on a wheel.

I walk past a man selling fruit under a big umbrella, the gutters behind him have been clogged with rubbish and now smell like rotting food.

I would advise him to sell his fruit somewhere else, but I don't think anyone minds. A black *Prado* stops in front of him, and a very light-skinned woman with rings on each finger rolls the window down and starts pricing the biggest watermelon.

I arrive at the laundromat finally. The signboard is old and washed, but if you squint, you can make out the 'Mama Abdul Laundry Services,' that was once painted boldly on it.

I walk into the reception and meet Halima at the front desk, where she usually is. Her eyes and face light up in the most beautiful smile you will ever see.

I stopped coming here because I hated seeing her (also because it was cheaper to wash my clothes myself), not that I had anything against her, just that she was almost always smiling. It upset me. I wondered what about this grim world filled her with so much glee.

That was old Austin. The Austin before the event. This reborn Austin still hates seeing her smile but is not going to make a big deal about it.

She's wearing her peach-coloured hijab today, and she smells like sweet spices. Her eyes are big and bright, and her eyelids are lined with kajal. I notice she has something that looks like a rash on her cheek, but I choose to focus on her lips instead as she talks.

"You just forgot about us," she says. "You found another place abi?"

"No, I just didn't have money," I reply.

She takes my bag from me and starts to count the clothes, making a face at how many they are.

"Mummy already said you can pay any time," she says as she lifts one of my singlets out of the pile.

"I know," is all I can manage to say.

"I've missed you," she adds.

I don't say anything.

✱✱✱

I'm walking home, nibbling on a pineapple slice I just bought. Halima told me to return my clothes tomorrow. I wonder if I'm spending the money I borrowed from my mother too recklessly.

I should have washed my clothes myself. It would have taken a decade and a few blood sacrifices for my ancestors, but I would have saved money.

"Where are you always running to?" I can still hear Halima's voice in my head. Something about that girl makes me uncomfortable.

I know I said my major gripe with her was her giddiness, but if I'm being honest, it's really the way she looks at me like she's trying to read my mind or the random things she says.

"You haven't looked happy in a while, Austin. You've been losing colour."

Who talks like that? I didn't go there for therapy, I went to get my laundry done.

I cringe as I think about how I stuttered in front of her, shrinking at the intensity of her gaze.

"I... I don't know... what you're talking about... I've just been busy," I had said, fiddling my sleeves.

Where am I always running to? Only place I wanted to run was out of that conversation.

I have missed her though, I hate to admit. Hearing her laugh at almost everything I said, made me remember when I moved here newly. I had brought a bag full of white shirts I ruined by soaking them with a pink towel.

I fell in love with her family. Abdul was a funny little rascal, her mother was warm and gentle, and I got along with Halima really well. I guess it was the way she laughed at everything I said, like I was the funniest person she had ever met.

I did my laundry there every week, even if all I had to wash was a pair of socks or a handkerchief or two, all because I needed an excuse to talk to her. One day, I stopped going. I've tried to tell you why, but I'm not sure I even have a reason.

Where am I always running? I don't know.

I finally make it home and sit on my bed again. I see that I have seven missed calls from my mum.

I call her and she answers before it even rings.

"So because you don't need money again, you have forgotten you have a mother," she says.

"Are you surprised?" I hear my father concur from a distance.

"Mummy, good evening."

"Where did you keep your phone?" she belts.

"I left it on my bed and went out to wash my clothes."

"You left your phone somewhere, you?" she asks in disbelief and starts to laugh. "Okay, thank God. It's today you decided to stop carrying your phone everywhere."

"Yes, ma."

"'Cause I refuse to believe you're the only person that has not wished your Uncle happy birthday because he corrected you last week."

"What?"

Today's my uncle's birthday?

I must have forgotten. I can see how this looks. My uncle called me last week and yelled at me for almost an hour straight, something about me being a slacker and not wanting to make anything out of my life.

"It's not that, I just forgot."

"So Facebook did not tell you?"

Facebook gave me a notification, now that I think about it, but I didn't pay much attention.

"Mummy I will--"

"And you don't say anything on the group chat, you don't talk to anybody. . . if you want us to leave you alone, just say it. It's only when you want money you start using your senses," my dad chips in.

I wait and duress-listen as they take turns reprimanding me.

"I'm sorry," is all I can manage to say. I want to tell them how sorry I am for being such a screwup. I want to tell them I'm doing my best to change. I almost bring up the symposium, but I keep quiet and listen.

"I'm sorry," I say again.

It's followed by silence on their part, and then they end the call. I sigh and rub my eyes. I immediately go to WhatsApp to leave a birthday message for my uncle and post a picture of him on my status.

It's a picture he took on one of his many trips to Dubai. He's wearing a white turban and looking directly at the camera with a frown. I still can't get over how unsettling his resemblance to my mother is.

My phone rings, and my heart skips a beat when I see who it is. I watch my phone, letting it ring until it stops. It rings again and I answer it this time, holding my breath until I hear her voice.

"Hello, Austin," she says, her voice as smooth and sweet as honey dripping down a broken comb.

"Hi Chinaza."

"Oh my God, Austin. I could not believe my eyes when I saw you called. What happened to you?"

"Nothing, I just wanted to talk to you," I laugh, picking at a thread sticking out of my bed sheet.

"I want to see your face," Chinaza says abruptly. "Let's switch to WhatsApp," The call ends and I wait for my phone to ring again. Soon, I see I have a video call request from her and answered it.

Her smile brightens one-half of my screen.

"Hey, Austin."

I smile and wave.

"Say something nice about my hair now, or I'll block you," Chinaza teases.

"Let me see it."

"I felt like doing twists today," she says, "I did it

myself."

"It's lovely," I smile.

She talks about things happening in her life, and my beating heart almost drowns out her voice. I wonder if now would be the right time to tell her how I feel.

I imagine how she'd react.

Oh my God, Austin, I just wanted us to be friends, but now you have ruined everything. How could you do this? You have brought about the apocalypse. The moon will fall, and the sun will explode. You have doomed us all. Why Austin? Why?

"Austin. . . Austin," she calls.

"Sorry, I spaced out there."

"So what I'm saying is not interesting?"

"That's not what I said."

"I'm too boring. You hate me, and you want me to die."

"Chinaza, you know I love you," I say.

She laughs and says, "Well duh, what will you do without me?"

★★★

It's five a.m. I'm jogging on the street for the first time in months. My thigh muscles hurt, my arms hurt, my body is covered in sweat, and I can barely breathe. I run through everything I have to do today in my head as cars speed past me.

I made a mental note to send my CV to a company

Linkedin recommended to me last night, plan to call my mother, and buy groceries with some of the money I have left. I'm still regretting not washing my clothes myself. I could have bought more food with that money.

When I get back home, the first thing I do is call my parents. I know they will be awake now for their morning devotion.

"Do you need money," my dad grunts.

"No, I just wanted to greet you."

He doesn't say anything for a while, then he grunts, "How are you?"

"I'm fine sir. Just went for a jog."

"You're doing exercises now?" I hear the surprise in his voice.

"Who's exercising? Austin?" my mum cuts in.

"Yes ma," I reply.

"Maybe you're finally learning to take care of yourself," she says and I hear my dad grunt a barely audible reply.

"I'm trying my best," I answer.

We talk some more and I tell them about my unsuccessful job search.

"I've told you, put your skills to good use, you are a smart boy, and you can create something for yourself," my father says.

"Or do you want to come home?" my mum asks.

"No ma, unless I'm about to die of hunger."

They both laugh at this. I can't help but smile.

"You will not die," my father says. "Don't worry, all of this will make sense eventually if you choose to be serious," he adds.

"Okay, sir," I reply, nodding like I'm standing in front of them.

"It is well with you," they say in unison, and we end the call.

★★★

Being unemployed gives me enough time to try to bring my *YouTube* channel back to life. I had managed to get two hundred subscribers, but I'm sure my absence would have trimmed it down a few.

I set my phone on my window, and sit in front of it, ready to record a video. I'm hoping the morning light will be good enough. I don't have a script, but I'm desperate to do something.

The recording took longer than I would have liked, but I managed to get through with it. I will edit the video later, but now I have nothing to do.

I go through my emails and find a few ads, something about my subscription to something expiring soon, nothing about how I've won a million dollars and I'm no longer a failure.

Maybe it's finally time to wash my bathroom. I walk in and immediately change my mind. I'd do it another time. I'm still not that brave.

But now, I realise, I don't know what to do with my life. I sit on my bed, listening to the compound rise with the morning and everything bursts with life: car horns, children laughing, school bus engines humming.

It's like a giant pause button has been slapped on my life, and all I can do is sit on my bed, as the world continues to spin. What if all this motivation leads me nowhere? What if I never get a job? What if I die alone, in this room? What if I get to heaven and God bursts out laughing because I'm one of his favourite jokes?

I lay on my back, watching a spider crawl on the ceiling until I fell asleep.

★★★

"My runaway customer," Halima's mum greets me as I walk into the laundromat. She's a short, slim woman, with a pair of round glasses balanced on her slim nose, reminding me of a kind Sunday school teacher.

"Good evening ma," I greet with a bow and offering an awkward smile.

"Runaway customer," she repeats. "You just forgot us."

"Ahaan. . . no ma," I try to sound sincere.

"He has found another place," Halima teases from behind the counter. Her mum laughs with her.

"Is that true?" Halima's mum asks, a suspicious glint in her eyes.

"Haba. Where would I even go?" I protest with

hands raised in surrender.

They laugh again and Halima hands me my bag. I can tell my clothes are inside, neatly folded.

★★★

I leave the house with my phone this time, so I can feel it vibrate in my pocket on my way home. I pull it out quickly. My heart flips in my chest with a heavy thump. I have a new email - it's a reply to one of the job applications I sent out.

I wipe my sweaty hands on my chest and open the I open immediately and. . .

Thank you for considering our establishment. We have gone through your application but. . .

I don't need to read to the end to know what kind of message it is. Another rejection. I take a deep breath and close the email, my chest heavier as I drag myself all the way home.

★★★

There was another speaker at the symposium that day, an older woman who spoke calmly. She talked about how the road to turning your life around will be littered with pain and disappointment. "Success is built on a foundation of many failures," she had said. I guess I just laid another brick of failure down in this building construction that is my life.

Getting Ls is nothing new to me, but it wouldn't

hurt to win something for once.

"I'm not a failure," I say to myself. I'm not sure I believe it.

I get home, put the bag beside my bed and call Chinaza. She answers on the first ring.

"This one that you're calling me twice in less than forty-eight hours, am I safe?" Chinaza jokes.

I smile, despite my despair. "Sorry for disturbing you, it's just that talking to you helps me feel better."

"Are you good?" Chinaza asked, her voice softer.

"Yes, I think," I hesitate. "Hey Chinaza, do you hate that most times I call you, it's because I need help or something?"

"I don't think you only call me when you need help."

"That's not what I said," I reply, suddenly uncomfortable. I take a deep breath and turn my neck until I hear a satisfying crack. "I want to do better," I say, "I'm trying to be better," I confess.

"I know," she replies.

I wonder if this is the time to confess my feelings.

"Chinaza. How would. . . imagine I tell you. . ."

"Tell me what?"

"Nothing. How have you been?" I say quickly, laughing nervously.

"No don't do that, tell me what?'

"Nothing really," I laugh again.

She groans. "I hate when you do that."

We talk some more and I end the call. As I hang up, I see my mum has sent me ten thousand naira. I text her heart emojis and say thank you.

Power comes on for the first time today and I plug my phone. I open the door to my bathroom and observe it again. I take off my clothes until I'm wearing just my boxers. I pick one of my old sponges and pour detergent on it.

Maybe, I will have to lose even more before I start winning anything. Maybe, I will never be brave enough to tell Chinaza how I feel. I can still work towards being better, I can still do the little things I'm brave enough to do.

I start scrubbing my bathroom walls. I rinse off a section and it almost looks brand new.

I get on my knees and scrub the floors, removing the yellow stains that have plagued this place for far too long. The world might be moving without me, my parents might be disappointed in me, but right here, right now, I can clean my bathroom, and maybe one day, all of this would make sense.

Ehiorobo Derek is a versatile writer, poet, and spoken word artist whose work has been featured in several literary platforms, including *Praxis*, *Poetry Column-NND*, and *Liquid Imagination*. His poetry has also been published in anthologies such as *How to Fall in Love* and *How to Fall in Love Again*, both released by Inkspired Nigeria.

Derek connects with a growing community of literary enthusiasts on Instagram, where he shares his thought-provoking poetry and creative musings.

Tito

Adeboye Kanyinsola

I snatched a lady's bag and started running down the crowded streets. I could hear the woman screaming and shouting:

"*Ole! Ole! Ole"* Thief! Thief! Thief! Save me!"

I heard people from a long distance helping her to shout it in Yoruba.

I made a sharp turn and kept running without looking back. I saw the fence I have made holes in. I use it as steps to fly over. I jumped and walked casually to the general toilet we shared with my neighbours; when I say 'we', I mean my parents and my sibling, Asabi.

I opened the bag I had just collected from my customer and saw one two hundred naira, two ten naira and seven five naira notes. I stared at it with disgust. This woman is broke and shouting like she has ten thousand naira inside her bag. What if those mob chasing me had caught me? They'd have burnt me to the ground because of two hundred and forty-five naira; that's just bizarre.

I put the money inside my boxers and took the bag inside. I can still sell it to Iya Shaki, my neighbour. We stay in what Nigerians living in the rural areas call 'face-me-I-face-you' also know as 'face-me-I-slap-you'. And it is a mad place to be.

You can't leave your food in the general kitchen or passage for fifty seconds. Why? Your food and pot will disappear together. If you want to wash and spread your clothes, just make sure you are at home throughout that day because, just like you guessed, they will fab it.

The *face-me-I-slap-you* house where I reside is unpainted. It has a balcony that's just five feet wide and thirteen feet long. And there's always a standby bench on the balcony.

The walls are not good-looking, and the toilets and bathrooms are in the backyard, not too far from the kitchen.

There are five rooms on the right and left, making ten.

My parents rented two rooms and merged them.

The door was facing ours. That's where Iya Ibeji

lives. Iya Ibeji has two sets of twins, and she is not the problematic type; she leaves the house and comes back before the house curfew, while Baba Ibeji hardly comes home.

The next room after ours is where Brother Kelechi Onishina lives. He is a fornicator as far as I am concerned- every time, there's always a different girl for a different day.

After Kelechi's room comes Iya Shaki. She would have been a fashionista, but her lack of education and respect is her problem. Iya Shakiru, known as Iya Shaki gave birth to Shakiru, an addicted smoker. Iya Shaki has two colours: a fair face and neck, burns on her cheekbones mixed with green, and the veins on her hands are visible, giving out some greenish vibes; her knuckles are dark, and her legs are black.

Then, Aunty Veronica lives in the last room on my line. Aunty Vero is wicked, and I can't blame her. Her name sold her out - 'Vero is wicked'; that's what her name means in Yoruba (Vero ni ika)

Back to Iya Ibeji's line. After Iya Ibeji, it's Baba Eleran's room that's next. He is a very violent man that doesn't joke with his knife. He told us to call him Mr Kunle and not baba Eleran. Followed by Iya Tawa. And like us, Iya Tawa joined two rooms because she has eleven children, and I don't know any of them by name. I only know Tawa, the first child and daughter of her mother so the rest of them go by the name Aburo Tawa (Tawa's younger one) as far as I am concerned.

The last room on the left line appears to be vacant.

***

On getting inside, I saw my sister applying makeup on her face, jamming different colours together like the Ayetoro girls from *Jenifa's Diary*. I cleared my throat and made for the room.

"Yes?" she asked. "Where are you coming from?"

"And where are you going to?" I shot back.

She gave me an unpleasant look and hissed, making me look like a clown.

She came into the room and started searching her bag, emptying it and refilling it.

She gave me this suspicious look that I didn't understand.

"Tito, where's my money?" she inquired, flaring.

"Me, I don't know, oh, you better lemme alone!"

"You'll think I am joking. Give me my money," she said in Yoruba, slightly raising her voice.

"I am not with your money, and what do you need money for garri?"

I knew it was about to go down.

She took the bag I brought in, took matches from the cupboard, dashed outside and set it ablaze.

By the time I got outside, it was already too late. The bag was already shapeless. Such ruthlessness.

"You know your money is inside that bag," I lied.

"It is a lie," she shouted. Then I gave her an all-knowing look. She does not know if she should put out the fire or come for me.

I smirked and ran away, leaving her crying over an empty bag.

I spent the two hundred and forty-five naira wisely, or I thought I did. I bought one dry gin and later used the change to buy bread and gari with sugar.

My parents don't have time for Tolu, my sister, and me. Tolu indirectly brought me up. Tolu taught me that taking things from people is not bad. That's what we do for a living. I know Tolu collects money from men, or men give her money, and I don't know why.

Iya Asabi and Baba Asabi, my parents, are wonderful people. Iya Asabi sells dry gin and herbal bitters for a living. Baba Asabi uses our ram to compete with other people's ram. I call it the 'game of horns'.

Game of horns, people will form a big circle large enough for two rams and start cheering the rams.

The rams come at each other with their horns.

They take steps backwards, like gathering power on their way back and then charging forward. The ram that escapes from the circle or surrenders loses the match.

They bet a lot, a lot on this game.

Baba Asabi, my father, is also known as Baba Landlord.

★★★

It was Monday morning, and I saw other students going to the same school as me, Onigi Grammar School.

I don't have many friends. I understand that school is a scam, although education is not. I don't like going to school. I know you'd say it is normal due to my nature. I did my research, and even the most brilliant students don't like schooling.

School is good; I am not saying it is not good, but at the same time, you can't say it is good. School is all academics, nothing more. I saw Shola, my friend, coming from the opposite direction.

Shola is a young lad, well built, five-feet-six just like me, and unlike me, he had no scar on his forehead and no cut on his lips from foul play.

We slapped hands and greeted each other. We got to the bus stop and hailed a bus.

We got to school early, and the school assembly started at 7.50 am. We strolled into the school at 9.00 am, that's awfully early.

Today, like every other school day, Mr Ayedun taught maths, and I don't know how Pythagoras' Theorem looks so complicated and why Mrs. Apata keeps preaching the gospel in a Home Economics class, and why they replaced our beautiful English teacher with Mr Sanyasi, using his native language to teach us compositions.

The timekeeper rang the bell for the break period, and we were on the field with no teachers' supervision. We scaled the deserted fence at the back of the school. When I say 'we', I mean Shola, my sidekick, Obi, the supplier, and David, that looks like Goliath, our bouncer. When we got to the other side of the fence, it happened to be close. We walked some more and saw a bench and sat on it. Obi, the supplier, brought out cigarettes for us to smoke. I hated cigarettes, but I didn't want to look like a weakling to my boys, so I took to smoking. We were still smoking when two police officers came.

I knew it was a lost cause when we were already inside the police vehicle. Goliath was already crying like the Israelites were weeping when they were between the Red Sea and the Egyptian armies like it was his last day on earth. This David has lost in both ways. He doesn't have the pride that Goliath had to prevent him from crying in front of his mate, and David doesn't have the Holy Spirit to comfort him. I gave him one last look and shook my head.

I just looked away and kept an expressionless face like I didn't care about what was going to happen. I just knew somewhere inside of me that today was not right; I went to school early today and was arrested. Satan comes in different forms, sha.

When we got to the station, they dragged us like goats into the station, and we saw a lone police officer who happened to be my aunt. I have seen her at my house a few times.

One day, I saw her sitting in my house on the couch for the first time. I just stood there amazed, thinking it was my mom speaking English coolly and not screaming at me in Yoruba.

Unlike my mom, she did not shave her eyebrows and replaced them with eye pencil and eyelashes with kohl.

She was wearing a gloss on her lips and not red lipstick. She didn't have a red blush on her cheekbones, just her face. Then my mom came in, and she was screaming just like she used to; I knew I wasn't dreaming for a start.

Aunty Bimpe's eyes fell on me. I looked away. She asked us to sit on the bench and asked us what had happened. I didn't have the mind to. Shola spoke on our behalf, said we had to get things outside the school, and the authority won't allow it, and we were on break and all those things, but he omitted the part about the cigarettes.

Her junior, the officers that brought us in, told her what happened, and then she gave me a look, the type of look Adam would have given Eve when they got kicked out of the garden of Eden.

She detained us till school closed and told my friends,

"The next time this happens, I will take you down to school and make sure you are expelled." She gave me a pointed look. "Y'all can go. Tito, you stay."

I was not afraid until this very moment; I didn't want to remain with her. I felt little to no guilt, but now guilt was now visible and had decided to cling to me.

We left the police station at around six. Another police officer took over from her. He didn't seem happy, but he had to come anyway. My Aunt, Aunty Bimpe, called my mom to tell her I was with her. We got to a kiosk and bought Fanta for herself and *Caprisun* for me; it took all the energy I had left not to slap it away from her hand. We walked a little bit more and we got to a canteen where she bought rice, dodo, two meat and one fish inside a nylon bag to take home. She bought food for me too, but mine lacked meat and fish; she bought an egg for me.

We scurried away and took the bus from Obalende, and then it dawned on me that she was going to my house.

"Omo Omo Omo, wetin dey sup what's going to happen like this," I was starting to question myself.

The lecture started when we got to the streets and had to stroll down a few yards before getting to my abode. A five-hour lecture was delivered to my ears in five minutes, the same amount of time it takes for me to get to my compound, and I can assure you that it was the longest five minutes of my life.

When we got to my house, she ordered me to bathe and change my clothes as if I didn't have personal hygiene. After I was done, I tore up the nylon and poured the food onto a plate. I helped my Aunty do the same and gave her water to drink.

She doesn't stay with us; she stays at Alausa, but I have brought her down here.

After the food, she kept on staring and giving me your-head-is-too-big-for-your-neck look.

My Aunty started talking again, scolding me silently. She kept on telling me about morals and rules and regulations, what or what not to do. She kept her voice down because my parents were now home.

My mom came inside with a pot steaming.

"*Ki lon'ba Aburo e so?* What have you been discussing with your nephew?"

"Nothing much. I am just telling him about my secondary school days." Aunty Bimpe smiled sweetly.

"O'da o. Okay o," my mom said, walking away.

Some minutes later, Aunty Bimpe told my mom she would be on her way; my mom screeched, "Let me see you off, Bimpe."

Aunty Bimpe looked at me and said, "The next time your mom reports you to me, or you are arrested, or you get caught doing *things*, you'd have yourself to blame - you just have to bid your life goodbye and be detained throughout your teenage years," she said through a stifled smile. I know she is threatening, but that's not polite – a Nigerian adult never threatens, they warn.

My mom came out just immediately after she finished what she asked, "What are you people talking about since?"

"It's nothing, Sister *mi*."

I slept on my side that night thinking about how I had messed up and had a big debt to pay for having my secrets on their palm. It felt like blackmail that didn't involve money but having to be well-behaved, and that's just beyond me.

Asabi is lying on the three-sitter chair, and I get to use the two-sitter as my bed.

Asabi was busy snoring, probably dreaming that she would tie me up and torture me or whatever she was dreaming of, and all I know is that I was in it.

I couldn't sleep. I sat up and rested my legs on the table. The old plasma TV was placed on a settee handed down to my dad from his dad, my grandfather. There were discs and cassettes of old movies and music, albums from Alhaji Sikiru Ayinde Barrister, Jesse King, Obesere, and even Fela. My mom was one of the girls who used to dance for Fela Anikulapo. I have a distaste for Fuji and high-life, hip-hop and R&B; those are my things. The thoughts of Aunty Bimpe's words seeped into my mind, and my heart did a *porrrrn porrrrrn*, skipping beats endlessly.

What have I done? I kept questioning myself, I was sure I was up all night, and then NEPA brought the light at around three in the morning. I saw it because we had not switched off the socket, and the clock was close to the ceiling, held to the wall using a nail. I stood up, turned off the lights, and turned on the fan.

As I lay on my 'bed', I realised I needed to sleep, join up the assembly, and dub my assignments, and this was just it. Living my life upside down, I don't blame anyone for misfortune or predicament. If anything, I blame myself. I have been a clean guy during my twelve years in this world.

I know my being introverted is unbeatable, yet I was called Pablo, I was nicknamed Jagaban, and all manner of nicknames in secret. The teachers say I am a good person, and the neighbours say to my parents in Yoruba, 'this your child is gentle' only Kelechi can testify against it.

I remember one time when Asabi told me Kelechi was disturbing her. I told her that she should not bother me. I executed my plan and showed Kelechi pepper, red scotch bonnets. I got lots of cockroaches, filled his room, passed water into his room, flooded it, poured sand inside his soup, and added devil bean powder to his bath water. Asabi came to tell me he had stopped disturbing her and that he even gave her money, begged her endlessly, and started avoiding my sister and me altogether. I didn't know the last thing I thought about before I fell asleep, but I woke up 7 am.

I stood up, took my bath, went to school, and joined the assembly; that was the beginning of my life. I did assignments and tests, and Shola was more brilliant than I thought; he helped me with schoolwork and everything else. Yes, Shola turned a new leaf with me, and I knew Shola was the best friend I could ever have.

Goliath, I mean David and Obi are still friends with us, but they still do their 'bad boys association', but it wasn't like before.

This 'good boy' I turned to didn't take away kleptomania habits. I grew up doing it. I try suppressing it countless times, but I still take erasers I don't need. I apologise to my Aunty Bimpe every time in mind. I only hope it gets to her.

"I am sorry, Aunty Bimpe. I hate taking things too."

★★★

JSS3 second term came, and I couldn't find my money; I didn't know if it had dropped or someone had misplaced it, but I didn't know what had happened to my money. I got to my bus stop late because I trekked. I spotted a lady afar off holding her bag carelessly behind me. I begged for pure water, rinsed my face, prepared my energy, ran through her, and took her bag. She didn't even shout or do anything. I kept running. No one is shouting. No one gave me a hot chase.

I scaled the fence, adjusted my clothes, dabbed my sweat and made for my parents' door. Only for me to open the door to find Aunty Bimpe sitting and sipping cold *Fanta*.

The first question that came to my mind out of the remaining one thousand I had was, 'what was she looking for?' I lost my tongue as she was smiling and talking to my mom.

"Can't you greet?" was what my mom used to greet me.

Oh, I found my tongue. "Good afternoon, ma. E ka san Aunty."

"Good afternoon," they screeched at the same time in Yoruba.

Aunty Bimpe's eyes fell on the bag clutched under

my armpit. That was the Oops moment.

Oops!

"That belongs to me," Aunty Bimpe said, no longer smiling.

My mom kept staring at us like she didn't understand Yoruba.

"Ma?"

"Where did you find my bag?" she asked, smiling again, her expression like NEPA's light unstable.

"You collected it from me, remember?" she continued. "You said you needed to catch up with a friend and that you'd meet me at your house in a few minutes."

"So you've seen Aunty Bimpe before and were acting like you are just seeing her for the first time today." My mom obviously didn't know what was happening, and I knew Aunty Bimpe was covering up for me.

I had a quick flashback. The lady is wearing the same colour of clothing as Aunty Bimpe; the lady didn't shout at me, the lady is Aunty Bimpe, and Aunty Bimpe is the lady.

Hello, Juvenile.

"*Sister mi*, I can take him with me now?"

"Oh, yes. Lemme pack some of his clothes for you."

Okay, here's the last piece. She had been planning my staying with her for a very long time, too, and I played right into her hand.

"Are you aware you took my bag some time ago?

Making me stranded, I had only two hundred and forty-five naira to take me to my place of work," she whispered to me when my mom went into the room.

I sat on the chair or collapsed on the chair. All I knew was that I was on the chair.

"That was how I became a part of y'all." I smiled at my inmates, my juvenile mates.

We were to tell our stories because today would be my last day at the centre. I am now sixteen years old.

The Unforgettable Christmas

Iquo Inyang

The war between Nigeria and Biafra had just ended. Everyone who had run away from Port Harcourt to Owerri and Umuahia were beginning to find their way back. Port Harcourt was a woeful scene of houses without roofs or partial roofing and mostly no windows or doors, walls filled with holes, bullets, and debris. Wherever you could excavate debris, and mortal remains became yours for a dwelling. There was no real source of right and wrong; people grabbed and secured whatever they could.

Mama secured a good-sized building with two bedrooms on the ground floor plus a garage. The upper floor was empty and with barely any walls left. It was enough for our family of six girls and two boys.

Hunger abounded.

Uzonwane, the Ada of the house, was a go-getter; she did the 'attack market' during the war and joined the Win the War Caritas and then the Red Cross Movement after the war. This movement came with weekly supplies of provisions and condiments for food; there was no money anywhere.

Mama also, in her wisdom, became a distributor to the only existing retail outlet, UAC (United African Company). The garage of the house became a store to sell most of these items. The house was overly full, with four older sisters, and the next thing to do was, as Mama put it, 'at your age, I was married to your father'.

This pressure for marriage was so intense that it was an obvious palpitation in all of us. On me, because my sisters would pick on me. Even Igwe, my elder brother, because he always took Mama's side of the argument. This trepidation became part of us on the way home from the sales of whatever was our chore for the day. Like a prayer answered, all but two of my sisters, the first and last two, that is, got married within a year. Unfortunately, my most annoying sister, Uzonwanne, wasn't one of them.

The state government finally found its feet and started proper governing. New laws came. One of which was about the occupancy of seemingly abandoned houses. One had to pay or purchase from the government. It was very political, and schemers schemed us out of our home.

We were left with one option: go to the village. We were not pleased with heading for the village. It took some getting used to. By the end of the week, life in the village became seamless. Although it was harmattan season, the weather was dry and scorched, so we ended our day with a wash in the stream. We learned how to dive after gulping water through our noses. We learned how to roast corn, pear, catch falling udala, and climb an orange tree without breaking its fragile branches. At night, we joined the gatherings for tales by moonlight.

Mama was uncomfortable with our relationship with the villagers, but she soon let us be. The freedom lasted only two days because she started a *mama-put* centre the following day and being the only boy in the house, I was expected to greet customers. Mama specialised in bushmeat, fresh fish pepper soup and nkwaobi.

I began to notice that Mama was sad. She was not only sad, but she was also lonely. There were no telephones and then the letters never came. Igwe, my elder brother, had been sent abroad with the dowries from Eziuzo, Ezinne, Ugwe. Uwa's dowry, which was supposed to be saved for me, had been used to take us to the village.

Mama would count the money she'd earned at the end of the day and sigh. She would raise it over her head with open arms and put it in a tin box and tuck it under her bamboo bed. I still wondered how Mama could sleep on that hard bed and not feel pain, like us. One day, I heard Mama talk to herself, 'one naira for… five naira…. How will I get bushmeat for tomorrow…" then Mama walked up and down, and you could hear her because she scrubbed the ground with one leg – that was how we knew Mama was still awake.

One day, I was called aside by a man who had come with a few friends. He had money because he paid for everybody's food and beer. The man wanted to speak to my sister, Uzonwanne, the annoying one. He was going to pay me two hundred naira just to speak to my sister.

I couldn't believe my annoying sister could be useful for something. If I get my sister to him, she could marry him. I'll have peace, and I'll still have two hundred naira so that we can eat chicken with rice and stew on Christmas Day. Also, Mama won't need to work on Christmas Day, which was over eight days away.

It was a good idea, I agreed. Knowing how annoying Uzonwane could be, I didn't tell her why I needed her help. But as soon as the man gave me the money he shouted:

"Take her!"

"Ewo'o!" I exclaimed and shouted: "Headhunters!" Then something hit the back of my head, and I fell. When I woke up, we were in a tiny hut. Everyone in it was covered in mud, including my annoying sister. The man closest to the door was tied up; he looked mad because saliva dripped from both sides of his mouth, and he bared his teeth.

Uzonwanne, my annoying sister, eyed me.

"I didn't know o! He just told me he wanted to speak to you."

"How much did he pay you?"

"Two hundred naira."

"Stupid boy."

We heard: 'kaboom' twice. We ducked and covered our heads with our hands.

"What is happen outside?" a woman cried.

"I don't know o," a gruff voice responded. "But I smell goatmeat, and I am hungry."

I looked at the madman and swallowed spit. My annoying sister smelt of goatmeat; she was still cooking it when I called her.

"This is your fault and your longer throat," My annoying sister said and hissed. "If I lose my chance of getting married tomorrow, I'll kill you and bury you, and our mother will never be able to find your body."

I believed her. Even though I didn't understand the talk of getting married, my annoying sister has never been known to say anything she didn't mean. Also, she was strong like a man. I swallowed. I now understood why Mama made me use lime to clean the rust on her George wrappers; I didn't know she was getting married.

"Fire!" a voice shouted from outside. Other voices followed.

"Where them?" a voice shouted from outside, and something crashed. A few minutes passed, and the door of the hut they were in fell in, and a man danced in with a shining cutlass in his hand. He took my annoying sister's hand, and I shouted.

"Ey leave her o! Take me instead."

The man sneered at me and asked, "Why?"

"Please don't use my sister for rituals."

The man with the cutlass grimaced and turned his head and shouted, "Are they complete?"

"How did you find us?" My annoying sister asked the man who was now loosening the rope around her wrist.

"Uzò's *ashewo*, the one with one eye and walks funny." the man said and lifted my sister and stared down at me. "She directed us."

I was afraid to ask why he kept an eye on me.

"And it took this long?" my annoying sister asked.

I was expecting her to be happy.

"What if I was already cooking inside somebody's pot?"

I agreed with her. I swallowed spit before I could parrot and remind them by my presence that I was the one who put us in this mess.

"This is a forest. And I did not know you were missing," the man snapped.

My annoying sister stared coldly at me and mouthed, "I will deal with you later," then nodded. As if that wasn't enough, she folded her hands, ready to punch me. I shifted from her and steadily watched her hands.

"Let us go before their main Oga comes to waste us."

Waste us?

"Waste us?" my annoying sister asked.

"This people no be head hunter o! Them dey chop people."

"Ewe'eeee!" I cried out and placed my hands on my head. I could see thick dark clouds of smoke in my mind. I could imagine an oversized
pot with my head dancing on top of it and people laughing as it sunk to the bottom of the pot.

"Ngwa nu!" another man joined us with a few more mud-covered people.

They took us home safely. Uzonwanne, my annoying sister, got married the following day and didn't get to pound me as she had promised. But Mama made sure I was the only one breaking palm kernel for its nuts until it was time for school, and then she sent me off to boarding school.

Iquo Inyang is also an avid traveler and reader, finding inspiration in diverse cultures and ideas. Her skills as a speechwriter allow her to articulate complex thoughts with clarity and passion. As a natural cartographer, she believes that maps symbolize both the journey of life and the exploration of possibilities unbound by time.

Her enthusiasm for geography and geomorphology is rooted in her upbringing, influenced by her father's deep appreciation for the subject. Iquo's passion for the earth's landscapes and their transformations informs her worldview, shaping her understanding of both people and places. Whether navigating the intricacies of civil service or charting new paths in education, Iquo Inyang embodies a commitment to lifelong learning and an enduring fascination with the world around her.

The Missing Part

Agnes Kay-E

Argh! Ebere! I thought as I jumped out of bed. The noise she made was tormenting me so much that I didn't need a nightmare to stay awake. With just one day left to my final exam.

"Look here, I can't shout o! Bring money let me take you to the hospital."

"I don't have any money."

"Haba nawh! It's not that bad," Ebere groaned.

"You say?" I snapped, all of me glaring at her.

"Ebere, your eyes look white. You've been clenching your teeth since I complained about the noise. Let us go to the hospital because the Panadol is definitely not working."

"I'm fine," Ebere muttered.

Exhausted and defeated, I stood over her, fuming and thinking of another way to get through to her.

"Did you have a D and C?" I asked suspiciously.

"Eh!" Ebere exclaimed, rising and then doubled over in pain.

"Girl, this is bad. You have GNS four tomorrow o!"

"Is it tomorrow?"

I hiss my reply. Ebere was playing with fire. Dr Morrison Achebe is one of the most ruthless lecturers in Saint Ignatius, and I couldn't afford to fail. So I gathered my bag and went to Drayton's, a classmate's room.

I don't like going to his room even though I've grown to trust him because of the way he looks at me. He knows I'll bust his head with a bottle if he tries anything funny. Drayton never got drunk, unlike Jesus-brother who knew the Bible back to front but always finished the night with a stagger and a woman's hand around his arm.

Looking for a reason to stay awake at night, I asked Drayton tons of questions about our exam, and we ended up teaching each other until morning. When I got to my room, it was quiet; the window was wide open, and it was cold.

The room had been stuffy, so I understood Ebere's need to leave the windows open, but there was a pungent smell. I closed the windows to keep the smell out and stepped on something sticky.

I quickly turned on the light.

What did I see? Semi-dried puke on the rug. Oh, I was livid. I had to bribe my cousin with six months' worth of baking before she let me have that rug.

"Ebere," I shouted, but then I saw her sprawled in an awkward angle near the fridge with her eyes wide open.

My heart stopped for a little.

"Is she dead? Hey, which kin wahala be dis?" I mumbled as I inched closer to her. As I did, I wondered, what if she was dead and already had a ghost and if it would imprint on me if I touched her and then begin to haunt me instead of the person that killed her? So, I stopped midstride, pulled back, and screamed.

"Come o! Come o! Ebere is dying o!"

I found I couldn't move from where I was, and other students who came to check hung around the doorway. Those closest to the door pulled their clothes over their noses, reminding her of the putrid smell of stale puke.

That's not what is doing me. I was thinking of ghosts. Should I have left her in the room alone? I thought against it. I was still debating in my mind when the porter showed up. he looked around grimly, went out, and a long while later returned with a police officer, two nurses, and five campus security guards. Moments later, two campus security haphazardly towed the stretcher out of the room with the nurse shouting after them:

"Take am easy nawh!"

I wondered how that would be possible with the height differential.

I shook my head and turned my attention to the order fo the day. I had GNS at nine-thirty a.m., so I jumped out of the room, hurriedly took my bath, and made my way towards the exam hall.

It was only seven-fifteen, and my final exam was for nine-thirty, but knowing that lecturer, I wanted to be there early in case he set the exam an hour early so that people would *sought* him for a better score – any earlier, the halls would not be open.

I think I did well in the exam and was glad to have discussed the topics at length with Drayton that night.

★★★

I was walking back to my room, wondering about how good my score would be and if it would up my GPA, and someone poked me. I halted. I frowned when I turned around to find it was Sheila. I don't think that's her real name, but she said it was.

"How is Ebere?" she asked wearily; her eyes seemed to convey more like she had something else to say, so I decided to say:

"Go to the room and check in on her."

"I heard she was taken to the hospital."

"Was she?" I asked myself and wished I had joined the drama club in secondary school.

"Ah-ah! Is she not your roommate?"

"Is she not your friend?" I snapped back at her.

"I... I travelled, and I just...." Sheila exhaled heavily and waved her hand. "No worry. I'll go with you to see her."

"Mm?!" I blinked in surprise. *Since when?* We don't even talk to each other.

"So, how far?" Drayton asked, halting beside me.

"Drayton," I said as slowly as I tried to figure out how to withdraw, creating space between me and Sheila. She wasn't a bad person, not that I know of. I just get bad vibes when she is around and tend to avoid her. Ebere had queried me about it and has queried her back. It wasn't like the girl went to the same church as us or a student, I'd never seen her in class.

"Me and Drayton have somewhere to be," I said quickly.

"We do?" Drayton asked, brows raised.

"My boyfriend Drayton?" Sheila asked.

"Eh!?" Drayton exclaimed and pulled away from us.

"Since when?" I asked loudly in surprise.

Backing down, Sheila cajoled, "Someone cannot play with you?"

Drayton looked from her to me and back.

Sheila clapped her hand playfully. "So, let's go to your room first, and then we'll go to the place you and Drayton —"

Fire! You and who? It was then it dawned on me that Sheila knew something of Ebere's predicament. Whatever it was, I wanted to be at Borokiri, not Mile 1. I know I've been told that I've got a suspicious mind, but I don't care. Bad vibes are bad vibes.

"You can go ahead. She didn't come for the exams, so she should be in her room," Drayton said suddenly.

"You're not coming with me?" Sheila asked, shifting her weight from one leg to another between furtive glances.

"We have somewhere to be," Drayton said and took my hand in his.

A part of me was relieved, and the other part, self-conscious, had to play along until Sheila was out of sight.

We walked to the restaurant outside campus, where I pulled back from Drayton.

"Let's go back to the one we know. Besides, I didn't tell you I was hungry.

I knew if we sat together to eat, everyone who'd seen how many times Drayton had tried to woo me would assume we'd started dating. I wasn't even sure of my feelings for him.

"I will pay," Drayton said as he gripped my hand firmly. "Your stomach says you're hungry."

I wanted to argue, but of course, the exploitative part of my humanity growled in that instant.

I followed him. As soon as I entered the place, my mouth watered. Aroma after aroma assaulted my nostrils as they devilishly embraced me from all sides like a pungent air freshener.

I hesitated. I didn't know how much it would cost, but I knew it would be expensive, what with the type of people that flocked into it at noon and evening.

In the blink of an eye, someone appeared beside me, holding out a tablet. An Apple tablet as a menu. I swallowed. Thinking of all the plates we'd be made to wash if we couldn't pay for the food, I kicked Drayton's shin from under the table.

With a bemused expression, he said, "Order what you want."

Knowing the 'wahala be like bicycle' rule, I shook my head.

"If you don't order anything, I'll order for you as I don't want you to ogle my food when it comes."

Drayton! They may make us wash plates for a week. A month sef.

The waitress glared at me, and I clucked my tongue. Drayton placed the order when I turned and caught Sheila walking in with a man with broad shoulders and mean eyes. Instinctively, I said:

"Let's sit over there."

Drayton followed my gaze and nodded. It was semi-secluded, but I wanted to sit behind the man, and the back of the chairs over there would be my cover. I hoped Sheila would join him.

"It's more private on this side," Drayton observed, nodding.

I didn't answer him. My concern was no longer about the food but about Sheila's presence on campus. What if there was more to Ebere's illness? What if it had to do with Sheila? Was I safe

When the food came, I gawked at them, my mouth watering - fisherman soup, catfish peppersoup, goatmeat peppersoup, and roasted tilapia covered the table, leaving almost no space for the drinks.

This boy really wants to disgrace me. At least they'll catch us together. I'll make him wash more plates.

"So?" Drayton asked. "Which one are we eating first?"

I raised my head to meet his gaze and frowned at his raised brow.

"Well?" he urged and thanked the waitress who had returned with a basin of water, and the two behind her had drinks on their tray.

"Let's start with fisherman soup," I said. Who knows when I'll have it again?

"Wow! You're hardcore."

"How do you mean?" I asked, already washing my hands.

"Well, no starters first."

"Oh. There's a time and a place, and it's not the first time you've seen me eat."

He fell silent for some time, and I heard a ruffling sound from behind me.

"Well?" a raspy voice mumbled.

A shiver ran down my spine because I was certain

I'd heard this voice over the phone with Ebere when she assumed I was still asleep — she called my name several times, but I didn't answer.

"What?" Sheila snapped.

"Why are you here? Where's your friend?"

"She's in the hospital," Sheila said

"Go and make sure she tells no one."

"I can't. Not yet," Sheila said.

"Excuse me," the voice sounded more stern.

"She is in the hospital," Sheila said in a forceful voice.

"If she talks… hmn," the voice said, and it was followed by ruffling that I assumed was the leather of the chair.

"Abeg, don't threaten me," Sheila said.

Just then, the waitress who had brought her the menu earlier passed by. This was the second time the woman was rolling her eyes at her.

"Menu, ma," the waitress said.

"Ewedu, okra, egusi, only roundabout," Sheila said.

Drayton lowered his head just as a shadow was cast over us. Somehow, I wasn't afraid because Drayton was great at boxing.

"Aren't you paying for the food?" Sheila asked airily.

"Sort it out before you call me," the voice said, sending chills down my body. I sighed with relief when he left, and I almost choked.

"Ordinary food you can't even pay just be puffing your shoulder anyhow," Sheila griped.

Drayton raised a brow at me, gesturing. Knowing his meaning, I shook my head vehemently.

"I don't want anything," Sheila snapped.

The waitress who had glared at me earlier apologized to her and hurried away. Sheila hissed, her hoarse voice diminishing as she walked away.

"So?" Drayton asked, distracting me. "What is really happening?"

"I'm eating," I said to avoid talking about Ebere. I wanted to explain what had happened that morning, but I didn't want any distractions. Besides, as course rep, he'll need to get information on Ebere, but not before I finish this sumptuous meal.

"You know what I mean. I don't like this suspense."

I ignored him.

"You think she has something to do with Ebere's illness?"

He knew. Does the whole school know? Ha Ebere!

"Drayton, let's go before the waitress returns o! I can't wash plates, o."

Drayton laughed. "I've already paid."

I sneered at him because I didn't see him pay.

"They make you pay before bringing you your order."

"Eh! Why didn't you say that before?" I asked, then looked suspiciously at him. "How much?"

Drayton laughed heartily as he unfolded his napkin and then looked at me. "I could tell you, but you'd have to be my girlfriend first."

Be your girlfriend? Keep dreaming.

I hissed. But since two of my course mates got engaged last weekend, I've been wondering. I mean, Drayton has proved to be focused, hardworking, and kind, and I believe he has potential. Unlike Ebere, she believed potentials took men nowhere farther than the dreams of a drunkard.

I gathered as many toothpicks as I could gather, tried to lift myself, and sagged back in my chair. "Can we do take-away?"

"Why not? We can't let the rest go to waste."

I nodded in firm agreement.

★★★

As soon as I was able to lift myself, we went to his room to store the food in his fridge and then we made our way to the hospital. I didn't need to show an ID because Ebere's mother saw me first and beckoned me forward.

"Good evening, ma."

"Good evening, ma."

Good evening, my dear. Where have you been? I've been calling you all day.

I curtsied and introduced Drayton to shift the attention from me, but it only worked for a few seconds.

"Thank you for helping them get her to the hospital."

"You're welcome," I said, now uncomfortable, with

an almost firm hand on my arm.

"Please come with me. The doctor had observed some things," she started.

I eyed Drayton, and he gestured to me. I nodded, hoping he meant he'd be waiting for me.

I followed Ebere's mother sheepishly to the room where Ebere was and halted in shock. There were tubes stuck in her arms and on her chest, and there was an oxygen mask over her nose. I'd seen enough movies to know it wasn't good.

I felt bad for her, but with the conversation being overheard, I became more concerned.

"Perhaps the doctor will be in a better position to explain.

I look from Ebere to her mother, then the doctor, and back at Ebere.

"Has Ebere been anywhere lately?"

"I couldn't say for sure…" I swallowed as Ebere's mother eyed me suspiciously.

"Our projects are different, and I was assigned to each team who had practically left everything for me to do, so we've barely seen eye to eye for months."

Ebere's mother frowned.

It was mostly true between helping the other students, marking scripts, and reading for my exams. I couldn't possibly mention that Ebere, since last semester, had been partying and visiting night clubs, missing classes, and returning drunk a couple of times.

No be for my mouth wen pesin go hia sey fowl

shoot bird the mama fly, so I was silent while wearing my most puzzled frown and hoping it was working. This was one of the reasons I stayed out of trouble- if I start to say the truth, and the truth that I know is different from another person's own, what happens then? I've been beaten for 'what I didn't know' countless times. And as this, my best friend is in this state on that hospital bed, even if I was a fly on the wall in whatever event led to her present state, I will not confess.

However, I could shift the blame to Sheila, whom I had avoided. It was probably God's way of rescuing me.

God Abeg, na Your hand I dey. Help me again. Help me again.

"The doctor said she has undergone some surgery. He won't give me more details as she is old enough to keep her details private."

I blinked, surprised because every doctor I'd come across was maximum *tatafo*. How else did we know who visited them and what they visited for?

Ebere, you sef. See what you've done to yourself.

"Do you know if," Ebere's mother started, then shifted closer and whispered, "If my baby had done an abortion?"

"Jesus!" I exclaimed and pulled back from her, stumbling. "Mma!?"

"I don't think you do such things. I just thought maybe she was afraid to tell me and if she confided in you."

I shrugged. "We don't talk about boys."

"You still don't?" Ebere's mother asked in surprise.

I looked at her, confused. "After my stepmother beat me because of Ebere, I don't talk about boys."

"I see," Ebere's mother said with a small smile.

I turned away and caught Sheila, and just as she was about to duck or hide, I quickly pointed in her direction.

"That is Sheila, ma. The one your daughter has been going out with."

"Ah! Come, my dear."

I was relieved when a stretcher boxed Sheila in. Sheila glared at me when she joined us, and I tsked. I was ready to leave them, then remembered an old movie that Patience Ozokwo was in where a party left and was practically tried, judged, and sentenced before the party returned from the market and decided to stay put.

"Good evening, ma," Sheila mumbled.

"Welcome, my dear," Ebere's mother said just as two men walked in. It made me realise it was a big room.

"Madam, good afternoon, ma."

"These are the girls," Ebere's mother said, and the men produced their badges, chirping:

"Inspector Olise and my colleague here is Sargeant Tubonimi. You're both under arrest for -"

"Tamuno, eh!" I exclaimed before he could finish, my hands already on my head and a tin pan shaped like a bean clanked with the floor.

Drayton appeared by my side. I didn't even have time to ask him when he switched positions, and the men pulled out handcuffs from their pockets, walking towards us.

"Tubonimi, no touch my girl," Drayton growled beside me, startling me.

"What?" Ebere's mother exclaimed, and then the EKG machine began to beep erratically.

My first instinct was to run, but Drayton was blocking the space between me and the policemen.

"I'm sorry my dear," I hear Ebere's mother say and ease her hand off the machine.

"Oga Drayton, wetin you dey do for here? Sargeant Tubonimi bellowed and shook hands with Drayton.

Inspector Olise nudged Sargeant Tubonimi.

"Oga Drayton, na police work I dey so."

"If na police work, then show me the warrant," Drayton asked with an outstretched hand.

"Look here," Inspector Olise started impatiently. "This matter no concern you."

As Sheila and I pulled away from the police officers, Ebere's mother pushed us back toward them.

"Please, take them away."

"Mummy," a voice said so faintly that we wouldn't have heard it if the room hadn't fallen silent for a split second.

"Oh, my dearest," Ebere's mother cooed.

I stared at Ebere, and although I could be

sympathetic to her state, I knew that if I was arrested, my stepmother would never bail me, so I quickly said:

"Ebere, please tell your mother what you've done o! Your mother wants to arrest me."

"Shh," a nurse said, walking in, but I was already bawling. Moments later, Sheila joined me, but in a softer voice. I was desperate enough to shove Drayton's hands away when he tried to console me. I have stayed out of *wahala*, tried to give myself a decent name, and did not know what we were being arrested for. I wasn't going to toe the line of sympathy, after all. I can do that later.

I impatiently watched the doctor check Ebere and absentmindedly observed the nurse scribble feverishly on a notepad.

"Em," Sargeant Tubonimi started. "Your daughter has woken up. We should ... em.. how shall we say, hear from the horse's mouth if you…"

"Not now, my patient just –"

"Ah! No o! My life is on the balance," I said, ignoring the condescending gaze from the doctor.

"We would like to speak to your daughter," Inspector Olise said softly. "She isn't drowsy, so she'll be coherent."

"Be gentle. Her blood pressure is still high..."

I wanted to say, 'Mine is higher abeg,' but the policemen seemed to have calmed down.

Ebere's mother had been leaning against the wall and observing them, and Ebere was now sitting. The fact that she looked so gaunt in less than a day brought tears to my eyes. All the while, I wondered. 'Ebere, what have you done?'

The inspector brought a crumbled pad that could fit into his palm and a pen as he inched closer to Ebere's bed.

"Miss, what is your name?"

Although it was minutes before she spoke, it felt like hours. She looked as if she wanted to laugh.

"But you know my name. I was at the party with you, Sheila, Bruno Lawson and – "

"The actor?" I asked without thinking.

The policeman's glare clipped my lips.

"Well, I left that evening with Sheila because I had promised to –" Ebere looked at her mother and hesitated.

"Go on, it's okay. The doctor knows."

What does the doctor know? Me sef I want to know.

"Mummy, I'm sorry. I needed the money, so I agreed to be part of it. It's just some eggs for a woman who desperately wants to give her husband children."

"How much money?" the doctor asked, startling me; I thought he had left.

Ebere lowered her head. "Two hundred thousand naira."

"Only?" the doctor exclaimed in horror.

What is this man's problem?

"I..." Ebere started, stole a glance at her mother, and fell silent.

"I give you everything you need."

"I know, but it's hard. I want to be able to have ice cream or wear perfume once in a while…"

"Ice cream," Ebere's mother snapped.

"Children of nowadays, when did you do this process?" the doctor asked.

"Doctor Paul," another doctor, almost half the *tatafo* doctor's height, murmured, "I'll take over from here."

"Ma?" Doctor Paul started, then nodded. Another nurse hurried toward them with a sheet of paper and handed it to the new doctor, who went through it as if she were counting.

"What is today?" Ebere asked weakly.

"Monday," Drayton answered.

"Friday. I did it on Friday."

"Mrs Onochie, good morning. Can we run a few tests on you?" the new doctor asked.

"I beg your pardon, whatever for?"

"I believe these are part of your family," the new doctor said. "The test results have come in. Your daughter has no kidney. It's been days, and I'm surprised her body is functioning perfectly, but time is not on our side."

"Kidney," everyone in the room chorused in a shocked whisper.

"Olise, where did you take my daughter? She said you were with her," Ebere's mother said as she sauntered towards the inspector, who was already holding the collar of his shirt.

"Madam, you're assaulting an officer of the law," Sargeant Tubonimi said, taking Ebere's mother's hand off the inspector.

Ebere's mother spurned. "You are Sheila. Start explaining where you people went!"

The school security guards had arrived and formed a semi-circle around the entrance, except for the thin one making a beeline toward them.

"Madam, calm down. This is a student, and we can't accept any form of manhandling," the one that came to stand between Sheila and Ebere's mother.

"Get out of my way," Ebere's mother roared, startling everyone. "Who are you?"

"School security. We brought your daughter to the hospital."

"You let this happen —"

"Madam," the thin man said, raising a hand as if to direct traffic. "Be careful what you say next. As reps of the university, you defame us, you defame the university."

"What?"

I understood he meant defamation, but I didn't think he had the power to demand it.

"Ma'am, we were reliably informed that the police had come to arrest two of our students. We just want to see the arrest warrant."

"Eh!?" Sargeant Tubonimi retorted while Inspector Olise stepped back until he was firmly behind him and then began to poke him.

"Make we begin dey go," Inspector Olise said.

"The search warrant, please," the thin man stretched his hand out.

"E do. You've made your point," Inspector Olise murmured. "Make I pass."

"Don't let him go anywhere o," Ebere's mother cried.

We'd been waiting forever because I was hungry, almost as if I hadn't eaten earlier.

"Oya nawh. Where did you people go?" I asked Sheila, poking her.

"Chief Tamunoebiere's house."

"Ha!" Ebere's mother shouted and cradled her head.

"Chief Tamunoebiere, the minister of oil and gas, brother-in-law to the governor of Rivers State, our VC's second cousin?" Drayton asked softly.

"Yes, the one."

"I didn't know you knew people in high places. He is in this hospital."

"What!?" Ebere's mother squealed.

"How do you know?" Sargeant Tubonimi asked, eyeing him suspiciously.

"Celestia, wife of his former PA, wrote a carry-over course today," Drayton answered and turned to me. "You remember that girl who tried to sneak a piece of paper to Pappi's desk?"

The woman that almost most of us got in trouble with even though we didn't have *nje*.

"Ma, I swear I was sure it was only to harvest eggs,

but then I didn't see anyone, and it was odd that they wanted to operate in the house, but they said the woman was in a wheelchair and all the necessary equipment had been shipped in."

Sheila fell to her knees, hands clasped in a plea as she said, "When it felt odd, I told Ebere, 'let us go', but she insisted she needed the money, and Leo transferred the money to her. He didn't even give me a cut, I swear."

"Ebere," Ebere's mother began to weep.

"I was pregnant," Ebere murmured. "The doctor that was to get rid of it said I had to pay all the money upfront."

I was dumbstruck. I stared at Ebere; she didn't have a boyfriend. Could it have been that man in the restaurant? Now I wish I had seen his face.

"I didn't tell you because I didn't want you to start judging me," Ebere fired at me.

See as your mouth strong. He had to be a married man; why else would she keep it to herself?

"Who?" Ebere's mother asked in a steely voice, surprising me. "Who is the father?"

"Chief Tamunoebiere," Ebere mumbled softly.

"Ah!" Ebere's mother exclaimed, crumbling to the floor.

Drayton and I lifted her just as a nurse walked, barging into everyone in her path and smacking her chewing gum loudly and talking. I watched her and wondered if the hospital believed in confidentiality because she may not have mentioned names, but she'd described the people she was talking about to a T.

As she shuffled around Ebere and the machine, the police officers backed to a corner while I and Drayton took another with Ebere's mother, and the campus security, which had reduced to three of them, remained in the corridor.

The nurse prattled on while we waited impatiently for Ebere to tell us who got her pregnant and when because I knew she didn't have a boyfriend. By the time the nurse was done with checking Ebere, I knew two nurses were frolicking with one of the doctors, one of whom was pregnant, and the doctor in question was a married man with a heavily pregnant wife. Also, a student who had missed today's exam didn't have malaria, but an abortion gone wrong had led to sepsis. The kicker was the mention of a politician whose surgery was delayed because the doctor to do the surgery had been delayed in the UK, but they were trying to get a Professor Anderson Ibe to stand in for him. However, it was his wedding anniversary, and he had taken the week off.

What was on everyone's mind, I assumed, was that the transplant had not taken place yet.

Ebere's mother signalled Inspector Olise, who was gawking at the nurse the whole time she was bent down. He reluctantly followed Ebere's mother out, where they lingered until the nurse came out, and they casually walked behind her.

My mind told me this was the time to make my exit,

but as the busybody that I am, I stayed. Why? Because Sargeant Tubonimi has just asked Drayton if I was the girl he'd been in love with since year one. As if that was not enough, Ebere began to chant in her sleep, 'Stop, leave me alone. No! Stop, please.'

It seemed I wasn't the only one who didn't like that statement because we were around her bed in seconds.

Ebere jolted out of sleep, panting.

"Where you...." Sergeant Tubonimi asked softly as if he was afraid to know.

"Did he force himself on you?" Drayton asked, holding my hand tightly.

My heart was hitting my chest hard, and anger riled in me. We had pledged to keep ourselves until marriage. That journey was hard without a partner, but when Ebere began to get the attention of the boys on campus in year two, our pledge changed. I was more determined to keep my promise because my stepsister already had a baby when I returned home last semester.

It was made easier because I had garnered no admirers. By the end of the start of my third year, I finally had breasts that were no longer pina colada umbrellas stuck to my chest. The fear of my stepmother stopped me from reading M&B, much less talking about boys.

Ebere narrated how she met Sheila at the student union's end-of-year party. She'd discovered that they shared the same birthday and were born in the same hospital. From then on, they went to parties together through Sheila's boyfriend, a DJ.

One evening, the minister and his friends in the VIP lounge invited them to join him at his table. She was hesitant, but Sheila insisted. As Sheila's boyfriend had been called away, she didn't want to leave Sheila alone because Sheila had had too much to drink.

He offered to take her and Sheila back to the hostel. Ignoring her protests, he forced himself on her in the car, and she soon felt a sharp needle prick on her shoulder. She thought nothing of it when she woke up in Sheila's room the following day until she discovered she was pregnant and realised it wasn't an alcohol-induced hallucination.

Drayton's hand was on my shoulder while I cried with Ebere. While Ebere was pouring out her heart, Sheila must have escaped.

It was almost three a.m. when Ebere's mother returned with Professor Abang, who had retired in my first year. Everyone knew because he defied the police when one of them shot a student by treating the student's wounds on the spot. He shook hands with Drayton, and then Drayton whispered something in Professor Abang's ear, and instead of the man taking my hand, he pulled me into a hug, saying:

"Welcome to the family," Professor Abang said in a sing-song.

Ebere's mother held an oblong brown bag, a blue and white box that looked like a cooler and a long white pipe.

"Sargeant, I think it's time to leave," Ebere's mother said.

I couldn't tell if she was upset or calm. She turned to us and said, "You too."

"See no evil, speak no evil, hear no evil," Professor Abang said, touching his nose and smiling.

Before I could say anything, Drayton tugged me out of the room, and just as we stepped out, the curtain was drawn. Drayton held my hand until I got to the entrance. There was almost no one in sight. The usually bubbly space was quiet except for a woman cleaning a different hallway and the nurse at the entrance painting her nails. I remembered my room key had fallen when I raised my hands earlier, and I hurried back to Ebere's room.

"Mummy," I heard Ebere say just as I was about to draw the curtain open.

"My darling, I brought your kidney back."

I gasped into my hand, removed my noisy sandals, ran towards the exit, and stopped when I saw the nurse. I inhaled a few times, tucked my feet in my sandals, and sauntered as calmly as my trembling legs could handle toward the exit.

"I've called okada to take us to your hostel. I hope you don't mind that I'll be joining you."

Mind ke! After today! No part of my body is missing. No prison.

"I'll stay in your room until Ebere returns."

"How do you know she'll return?"

I wanted to tell him what I had heard but then thought – *no be for my mouth pesin go hear say fowl shoot bird the mama fly* so I shrugged.

★★★

It's been three years now. I married Drayton two years ago, and we're expecting our first child any day now. Drayton hadn't paid for the food that day because he owned the place. All the time, he came to I and Ebere's room to eat was his way of getting my attention. Interestingly, Professor Abang was Drayton's uncle on his late stepfather's side.

I've been thinking of Sheila since I set eyes on Ebere a couple of weeks ago. Did she turn out alright? Did she send herself into exile to avert that man's threat?

Maybe it was the fear of losing my virginity the way Ebere did or the fact that I may be the only virgin on campus; I'm not certain, but I decided to stay with Drayton.

Sometimes, I wonder if I'd ever end up with Drayton if things had not turned out the way they did, because his mother had turned up a couple of hours later with a girl she considered suitable for Drayton, but found me in Drayton's shirt in Drayton's bed. What if Ebere hadn't fallen ill that morning? What if she never got her kidney back? What if Ebere hadn't woken up before I was to be handcuffed?

The missing part was different for each of us.

For Ebere, it was hard to tell. Was her mother too strict? Was she simply greedy? Anyways, she's married to an oil tycoon now, they've two children and she's pregnant with the third.

Drayton said that each time I turned him down when he asked me out, it chipped away at his courage, so I'd guess his was his confidence.

Ebere's mother's own could be the secret she'd kept from Ebere, which resulted in her being pregnant for own her father.

As for Sheila, I'll never know.

For me… I'm still unsure.

For you, who knows?

Agnes Kay-E is an accomplished author of sixteen published books, spanning from adult fiction to children fiction.

She has, since November 2021, hosted weekly live interviews with African authors every Saturday on Instagram.

In addition to her writing, she has coordinated five successful short story competitions and two collaborative projects. Agnes believes the world is grim without rose-coloured glasses and hopes her stories offer readers an experience that feels like "the easiest hellos and the hardest goodbyes."

Contacts

Thank you for purchasing this book! I hope you enjoyed the journey. If you'd like more, feel free to connect with me at any of the platforms below. And don't forget to share your thoughts by leaving a review at your favourite retailer!

Facebook: https://www.facebook.com/kepressng
Instagram: https://www.instagram.com/kepressng
For newsletters: https://www.kepressng.com

About Us

At Kemka Ezinwo Press (KEP), we believe in the transformative power of African storytelling. We celebrate the voices of young, old, and veteran authors, each with a unique perspective, weaving tales that reflect the richness and diversity of African experiences. Our mission is to foster a deep connection between readers and their roots, producing books that inspire a sense of nostalgia for Africans in the diaspora while offering a mirror for those seeking stories that resonate with their lives.

KEP exists to amplify African literary works, combat stereotypes, and remind the world that Africans are avid readers and creators of exceptional stories. Whether it's discovering new voices or reconnecting with familiar themes, our books offer readers a journey of self-discovery, pride, and cultural connection.

With a core commitment to Excellence, Collaboration, Discovery, and Generosity, we create platforms for both emerging and established authors. Our vision goes beyond publishing; we strive to cultivate a community where African literature thrives, empowering readers and writers alike to embrace their identities and share their stories with the world.

At KEP, we are more than a publishing house—we are custodians of African narratives, shaping the future of literature while honouring the past.

Other KEP Titles

Ogu & Other Stories
Notes on Love & Other Stories
Rebirth
Flip-Flop
Oops!
Bound By Fate
Sink or Swim

2026 COMPETITION!

Attention all writers of African heritage - this is your moment to shine. The 2026 Kepressng Anthology Prize will officially open for submissions on May 29, 2026. Whether you're a published author or just beginning your journey, we invite you to explore this chance to showcase your talent.

Ten lucky winners will be published in an anthology. This year, the competition features four categories:

~ VINE
~ LILY
~ JUVENILE
~ OAK.

The theme for each category is the same as the title, but it's up to you to interpret it however you wish – literally, figuratively, or creatively.

GUIDELINES

Entry is free and open to all Africans and those of African descent.
~ Your work must be original, unpublished and not AI-generated.
~ Your entry must be in English and fictional.
~ You can submit only one entry per category.
~ All entries must be submitted in MS Word format, double-spaced in TIMES ROMAN font.
~ Your name must not appear in the body of the story.
~ The entry must be between 5,000 and 10,000 words.
~ Your submission email title must be as follows:
CATEGORY TITLE - YOUR STORY TITLE - YOUR NAME (PSEUDONYM).
~ All entries must be received by Midday of October 11, 2026.
~ The winners will be announced six to eight weeks after the last day of submission. (A Change of date will be communicated.)

This is an incredible opportunity to have your work recognised, gain exposure, and most importantly, join a vibrant community of African writers! We can't wait to see your interpretation of these themes. Send your submissions & FAQs to kemkaezinwo.press@gmail.com.

Good luck.

Made in the USA
Monee, IL
03 May 2026

49438541R00173